MW01613464

Your quotes are amazin
faith and the direction c
have learned so many t

– Jane Walker, Friend and member
of Women of Virtue Widow's Ministry

I, along with a lot of others have received these quotes daily. I post them on face book and receive scores of likes and comments from people that are blessed, inspired and encouraged thru these thoughts. A preacher once said "One thought from God, fitly communicated can transform a life; save a soul; heal a hurt and mend a mind". In order for it to do so, the word must be shared with those who need to hear it.

Sis. Betty shares what I call "God Thoughts" with people from all walks of life. Many have said her words have turned a "not so good day" into a blessed day. May all the world learn the power of God written or spoken through a yielded, humble, and obedient servant of God like Sis Betty.
May her thoughts and writings live on for generations to come through this compilation of her "Thought for the day".

– Jeffry A. Woolston Ordained Bishop, Church of God
(Cleveland TN), retired Pastor, co-laborer and friend.

Betty has inspired me for several years with her relevant and powerful sermons at the Wednesday morning services. Now she is blessing many people with her fun and interesting stories taken from her life. They bring back memories of times we used to enjoy. The Spiritual application she brings to these devotions touches our hearts and draws us closer to our Lord and Savior.

– Marilyn Moreland, Retired teacher and Pastor's wife

I really enjoy reading Betty's "Thoughts For Today". Betty came from hard working, dedicated to God, Christian parents. I love the way she shares things that happened in her family history when she was young and makes a Christian point that blesses the heart and soul of people with these Godly "food for thought". Keep up the good work in blessing others that need a spiritual lift.

– Elizabeth A Jones, PhD Christian Counselor

Thoughts for TODAY

"May each thought in this book bring encouragement to you as you read them.

Betty

by

BETTY COGHILL

ISBN: 978-1-64288-159-2

ALL RIGHTS RESERVED: No part of this publication may be reproduced, stored in a retrieval system, or transmitted in any form or by any means – electronic, mechanical, photocopy, recording, or any other – except for brief quotations in printed reviews, without the prior permission from the author.

Copyright © 2021 by Betty Coghill
All Rights Reserved

Printed by Derek Press
Cleveland, Tennessee

FOREWORD

Sissy, our little Maltese, loves to sleep in a sunny spot. Often times while sitting in my lift chair, I watch her through the day, move from place to place following the sun that shines through a south window.

Just as I watch Sissy follow the sun, for fifty years I have watched my wife Betty, follow the SON; always staying in the light of His love.

For more than a year while sheltering in from the Covid virus, Betty has sent out a daily "Thought For Today". These thoughts begin with a true story from her life; mostly childhood memories. Then quickly they transform into analogies which show what our Lord will do for you.

Betty known to most as "Sis. Betty" and to many as "Pastor Betty" shares these stories currently with over a 120 people; most of which share them with others.

Sis. Betty, which I am blessed to call "my wife", is driven to share the love of God with all she meets.

Sit back and enjoy these daily thoughts from a country girl. You will find many that will bring back memories of your own life. You will no doubt feel connected to this wonderful woman of God.

Michael Coghill

PREFACE

My name is Betty Coghill. I was born in Clarksville TN. My two sisters and I were raised by two Godly parents which taught us the values of faith and love. Because of them, I am where I am today, and excited to share these thoughts with you.

Being raised in the country, I have many memories of my childhood and often ponder on those who have made an impact on my life growing up. Every step I've taken has been led by my heavenly father and I love to share many of my life experiences through my thoughts, that I have treasured over the years. On each page you will see how I've come this far by faith; and how I have allowed God to lead and direct my steps.

As you read this book of devotions, my desire is that you will walk where I walked and your faith will increase with every experience I share with you. May you be inspired to trust our Lord in every experience you walk thru in life.

BE THE SPARK

Several years ago there was a song that said "It only takes a spark to get a fire going". It doesn't take much of a flame to spread and send out heat. My husband and I used to camp a lot. I remember one time we went to another camper's campfire. They had written a song about us. It's amazing how a "spark" of compassion; love, joy and God's Word can bring a "fire" of peace and faith to others during a difficult season in one's life. Take this time to draw closer to the Lord; and pick up your phone to text or call others that come to your mind. Let's spread more love along the way. You may be just the "spark" someone is needing today.

←————————————→

WHERE IS THE CHURCH?

I saw a sign posted that read "The Church has left the building". That sign made me do a lot of thinking. We may not be in a church building; but the church consists of you and me. We're the body of Christ. God speaks about His church: "upon this rock I will build my church and the gates of hell shall not destroy it." No attack of the enemy can come against or harm it. "Greater is He that is in us than He that is in this world". We can rest assured where we are and the believers are, the Lord is in our midst. He is right there with us. I'm glad to say the Church is alive and well!

←————————————→

MISSING IN ACTION

We all have family and friends that are out of town; even miles away. I personally miss the time and fellowship with them when we can't be together. We desire so much to be with them during all the chaos going on in our world today. We miss the closeness and fellowship with our brothers and sisters in the Lord; and our time of meeting together. These people may be missing from our daily contact; but the Lord is never missing. He said He would "never leave us nor forsake us." So in this moment, get to know and fellowship with Him like never before. He's never "missing in action" in this pandemic. He's always there.

STILL SMALL VOICE   4

Some people are very soft spoken. I, for one have a loud voice and can be heard from a distance. In 1st Kings 19 we read "the Lord passed by not in the wind, nor the earthquake, nor fire, but in a still small voice." I encourage each of us to take time each day to focus away from the media; but to God so we can be quiet and listen and know "that God is still God." It is thru His "still small voice" we can hear from Him and experience joy, peace, and refreshing that only comes from Him during this season in our life. Be encouraged in our Lord. In the midst of it all, His still small voice can still be heard.

NEVER CLOSED   5

I felt as if our world had come to a stand-still. I remember there was very little traffic on the road; and the restaurants were closed to inside dining; all because of the pandemic. Even schools had closed. The business world and individual families were affected by all these closures. But God's love, protection, ears and heart are never closed to His children. Psalms 34:15 reads "the eyes of the Lord are upon the righteous and His ears are open unto their cry." You will never find a "CLOSED" sign on God's door. He answers every time. In fact He's knocking; just waiting for the door to be opened.

EXERCISING OUR FAITH

Many people go to the gym regularly to exercise and keep in shape. My sister and I usually find us a place to walk, talk and get our exercise. When the gyms were closed, they had to find other ways to work-out at home. People know the more they exercise; the stronger they become. As Christians we need to daily exercise our faith; our praise; our authority; and God's Word in our life. Ephesians 6:10 tells us to "be strong in the Lord; and in the power of His might." Exercise is never comfortable; but it can help us become who we want to be. So it is with our relationship with God. The more time we spend in His word; prayer and with Him, the stronger we become.

THINK ON THESE THINGS

Often times I find myself sitting and thinking. I think about the blessings of the Lord and all He's done for us. Philippians 4:8 tells us how the way we "think" plays an important part of our day to day living. It says to think on things that are true, honest, pure, and just; and even things of good report. I admonish us to think on the positive not the negative; to look for the good and not the bad. Let's keep our minds on Christ. Who's report will we believe? Let's believe the report of the Lord. His Grace is sufficient to get us thru everything. "And the peace of God shall keep your heart and mind thru Christ Jesus." That's something good to think about.

FEAR NOT

8

Many years ago, I had a problem with some fear. I had to work hard to overcome it; but God helped me thru it. No one can say that fear is not real; because it is. In Luke 21 we read "men's hearts failing them for fear and for looking after those things which are coming on the earth." We can sense the fear among people we talk to. But God has not given us the spirit of fear. Don't let fear hinder your faith and walk with God . His Word declares: "Fear not for I am with thee; be not dismayed for I am your God." That tells me we have nothing to fear. God has got this and He has got our back. Friend when fear comes to your door, send faith to answer it.

WHERE CAN WE GO?

9

In John 6 we read many walked away from Jesus. So Jesus asked His disciples "will ye also go away"? Peter's response was "to whom can we go? Thou hast the words of eternal life.". In troubled times, people either run to God or away from God. I ask you "to whom can we go?" Friends there is nowhere to go but to God. Jesus said "draw nigh to me and I will draw nigh to you." He also said "I am the way, the truth and the life". Those are words of comfort for us all. Let's draw closer to Him. When a situation arises, go to Jesus. The old hymn says "Where could I go but to the Lord?" The only place I go when I need help or an answer is to the Lord.

THE BRIDGE OVER TROUBLED WATER

I'm not one that likes to walk across bridges; especially those suspension bridges that make you feel you are going every direction. They can also make you feel very insecure. The disciples were on the boat when a bad storm arose. They were afraid and went to the back of the boat to awake Jesus. He walked out and spoke "Peace Be Still" and all was calm. Things in life can cause a storm to arise in the heart of God's people. Many can feel shaken; afraid they are going to perish. If you are in that boat, let Jesus speak peace to you today. He's the bridge over troubled waters; and you will get thru this safely.

←——————————————————→

DELAY DOES NOT LAST FOREVER

There are times my husband and I order food from the grocery store to be picked up. Sometimes the pick-up day would be as much as 3 days later; but we waited patiently because we wanted the items we ordered. Sometimes we face delays in our life that we don't always understand. Sometimes our prayers seem to be delayed as well. Delay does not mean defeat. God knows what He is doing. Often times God has a greater plan for our life. We don't need to understand; we just need to hold His hand. The good thing about it is delay is not forever; because the bigger picture will unfold soon.

←——————————————————→

TOGETHER WE WILL GET THRU THIS

We've heard the saying "we will get thru this together". How true are these words. When I'm going thru something; it's great to know there are others that really care. No one should have to go thru things alone. We should be sensitive to the concerns of others. Jesus told us in Galatians 6 "to bear one another's burdens". I believe we should stand together in the good times and the bad times. But the best part is we always have the Lord to lean on. He promised "He would never leave us nor forsake us". With God's help we are going to get thru it "together".

NEARER MY GOD TO THEE　　　13

I'm one of those people that love the company of others. In fact I am not a loner at all. When our Lord died on the cross, we know He felt forsaken and alone. During the pandemic the words we heard often were "social distance". We couldn't gather in public places like we used to or get close. We had to be at least 6 feet apart. I'm glad these two words do not affect our relationship with God. We can be as close to the Lord as we want to be. The closer we get to Him; the bigger our God becomes; and the smaller the cares of this world seem. The best solution is to "draw nigh to Him; and He will draw nigh to you".

SWEETER & SWEETER　　　14

I look over my life and can say "this journey has been a good one" because I've found out "Tis So Sweet To Trust In Jesus". It's a beautiful hymn I love to hear sung. Many of us have trusted Jesus over the years thru so many situations such as our finances, health, and other areas of our life.　One thing we have learned is we can trust Jesus completely. He will not let us down. It's easy to trust a risen Savior who is alive! I'm thankful our relationship with the Lord is so genuine and real. The old song says it so well: "It gets sweeter and sweeter as the days go by".

A PRAYER OF SECURITY 15

All of us desire to feel safe and secure. I feel this is a prayer each of us could use every day. "Father, wrap your arms around your children; letting them feel secure and safe. Where there may be questions in their mind; let them know you are the answer they are looking for. Where there is fear; replace it with faith. Remind them you are fully aware of what is going on and nothing surprises you. Remind them they will get thru this; and they are secure in you. Give each one your peace and flood their heart with joy. Again, remind them everything is going to be alright".

←——————————→

SUPPLY NEVER RUNS OUT 16

During the pandemic we ordered groceries online several times to be picked up at our car. Some of the items we ordered online would be out-of-stock. I'm so thankful it's not that way when we make our request to God. Sure, the stores may be out of bread; but Jesus is the Bread of Life. He knows exactly what we need; but wants each of us to make our petitions known to Him. The Bible says "my God shall supply ALL your needs according to His riches in Glory". Just think: He owns all the cattle on a thousand hills; and all the tators under it. Pretty awesome. That tells me, Jesus is all I need.

←——————————→

TIME 17

Time: an important word in our daily living. We don't enjoy waiting; we want it now! Why is there a waiting period? During the "waiting period" we must look around and see what God wants to do in our lives personally. God doesn't want us to be concerned about time. Isaiah 40:31 says "they that wait upon the Lord shall renew their strength; they shall mount up with wings like eagles; they shall run and not be weary; they shall walk and not faint." Things may take time; but the waiting is worth it. God's timing is perfect. He's never late; but always on time.

I'M RIGHT HERE 18

I've heard the song "I'm Not Going Anywhere" and its words speak to my heart. It says "take my hand; don't let go….hold me close, hold me near; please let go of all your fears; I'm not going anywhere." Those words are powerful. I can hear Jesus speaking those same words to us. The song goes on to say "seasons change with no wind; but I'll be there until the end." Jesus will be with us all the way. He's definitely not going anywhere. He'll be right here. He promised in His word that He would never leave us nor forsake us. He'll be right here in our today and in our tomorrow. That's a promise we can always count on.

SOMEONE SPECIAL 19

Everyone wants to feel special. I remember how our parents made us feel that we were so special. There are people in our life that are so special to us; but do we realize how special we are to God? We were created in His image. In fact we are a "chosen vessel". We are "one-of-a-kind"; and no one can take our place. We have been bought with a price…the price of the blood of Jesus. In fact we are "blessed and highly favored" by the Lord. We are not who we "think we are" or what others "think we are"; but who Christ says we are. We are a royal priesthood; a child of the King; an heir of the kingdom. That tells me we are pretty special.

$$\longleftrightarrow$$

ROSES WILL BLOOM AGAIN 20

I enjoy beautiful flowers and trees in full bloom. They let us know our world is alive. I hear little birds singing as if to say "I'm not worried about a thing; I know my heavenly Father will take care of me." God will take care of us too. He wants to put a song in your heart as well. Don't focus on things unpleasant in your life. Oftentime we don't take time to stop and "smell the roses". You may not hear the birds or see the flowers now; but "Roses will bloom again; just wait and see-don't worry about what might have been; only God knows how and when. Yes, roses will bloom again."

$$\longleftrightarrow$$

A BETTER DAY IS COMING 21

All of us have days that are better than others. I think about the blessed hope we as Christians have. One day we won't be concerned about the cares of this life. John tells about it in Rev. 21. He saw the Holy City coming down from Heaven; where we will dwell with Christ forever. No more tears; death; sorrow or crying; these things will be passed away. We must not allow anything to take our "eyes" or "vision" away from what is to come. The hymn says "there's a great day coming…by and by." Let us comfort one another with these words: "Even so come Lord Jesus".

LEAN ON ME

I love the hymn "Leaning On The Everlasting Arms". Sometimes we long for a shoulder to cry on; or a rock to lean on. I recall the song "Lean on me when you aren't strong. I'll be your friend; I will help you carry on. We all need somebody to lean on." I'm thankful we have the Lord to lean on. I'm reminded of a missionary overseas; who was so tired after a service. While sitting on the ground in a hut a native lady came and placed her back up against the missionary's back; and whispered: "If you love me; lean hard". Today God is saying "if you really love me; lean hard on me."

WHAT DO YOU SEE?

An Art Professor asked his class to choose their favorite of two pictures. One was a beautiful scene of flowers; trees; birds flying in the sunlit sky over a beautiful lake. The other picture was the same; but with dark stormy clouds; trees blowing with heavy rain. Naturally the students chose the first picture; but the professor said he chose the second one. In spite of the storm; dark clouds and rain; he saw a little bird on a twig over the water, hanging on. That little bird would not let go. Friend hang on and don't let go. As the hymn says "Hold me close-let me stand; in the hollow of your hand. Keep me safe 'til the storm passes by."

TASTE AND SEE

I thawed strawberries I had frozen and decided to make jam. While cooking the mixture; I thought of our life.

We are a lot like this jam. The strawberries had to be tasty and in good condition. The sugar was to make it sweet; and the fruit pectin made it the right consistency. If we aren't careful our life will feel "jammed". You and I need a sweet disposition and the right consistency of love to pass on to others. As I poured it into the jars; I made sure to seal it properly. We must show the fruit of the spirit; have a sweet disposition; sealed with the Sweet Holy Spirit, so others can say "O taste and see that the Lord is good." Psalms 34:8.

A BLESSING IN THE MIDST OF WAITING 25

All of us want our lives to be of a normal routine; but often times God allows our life to be interrupted for a season. It's during this time-frame God can speak to us and bring blessings and peace. We must trust Him while we are "put on hold". Numbers 6:24-26 reads "the Lord bless thee and keep thee; the Lord make His face to shine upon thee; and be gracious unto thee. The Lord lift up His countenance upon thee and give thee peace." This blessing comes when we trust Him. And really that is the secret: just trusting Him.

SPREAD THE WORD 26

I heard the statement from one of our leaders "spread the word-not a virus". That's a good thought for each of us. Just as a cold, flu or virus is contagious; God's Word can be just as "catching". It can transform a life and bring hope to many. We are reminded of it in Jeremiah 15:16 that says "thy words were found and I did eat them; and thy words were unto me the joy and rejoicing of my heart; for I am called by thy name O Lord

God of hosts." Today is a good day for each of us to make a commitment to spread the word to others.
How else will others hear the good word we have in our heart?

HOW BIG IS GOD? 27

Have you noticed when we fly, the buildings, trees, vehicles, and people on the ground look so small? "How big is God" a little boy asked his dad. Taking his son outside, the dad pointed up to the sky. "Son how big is that plane?" The boy replied "very little dad". Later that day the dad took his son to the airport and went to a window where they could see an airplane outside. "How big is that plane"? The boy said "BIG!!" The dad smiled at his son "that's the way it is with God. The closer to God we are, the bigger He becomes in our life." He will be as big as we allow Him to be.

GIVE ME JESUS 28

The older I get, the more precious my relationship with the Lord becomes. I could travel miles seeing the sites-but I realize all this is temporary. I'm reminded of an old farmer who had never been anywhere. A good neighbor decided to take him to New York City. He saw the Statue of Liberty; ate in fancy restaurants; and saw many other sites. When he got home he was asked "how did you like the big city?" Being very serious, he replied "I guess it was ok, but I didn't see anything I couldn't live without." Friend-the only thing we can't live without is Jesus.

LIFE IS FRAGILE 29

I remember the day we got word one of our neighbors had gotten killed on his lawn mower. It brought home how fragile life is. The saying "life is fragile; handle with prayer" is so true. Things can change in a moments time. We should never take for granted that things will stay the same. There's a saying I've heard many times that says "only one life will soon be past-only what's done for Christ will last". Let's not get so engaged in day-to-day activities, that we forget what really matters most: a smile; a hug; phone call, text or even a card. Don't put off until tomorrow what you can do today.

$$\longleftrightarrow$$

THE WATCHMAN DOESN'T SLEEP 30

My husband's family has a coat of arms that reads "Non Dormit Qui Custodit", Latin for "he that guards does not sleep". I'm reminded how a shepherd stays awake all night and watches to guard his sheep from harm. I'm thankful we have a shepherd that stands guard every moment of the day and night; to watch over you and me to make sure we are safe. He never sleeps to watch over you and me to make sure we are safe. My advice to each of us is to go ahead and get sleep. There's no need of us and the Lord both staying awake all night. It's a great thought to know our watchman is pulling "guard duty" and never sleeps. He loves us that much.

$$\longleftrightarrow$$

A GREAT JOURNEY IN SPITE OF IT ALL 31

I love the saying "God never said the journey would be easy; but he did say the arrival would be worthwhile." Each of us want our travels in life to be smooth-sailing; but sometimes there is a few bumps and curves in our way that changes our entire routine. No matter how bumpy the ride is, I've learned the greater the challenge, the greater the victory. Let your "ups" and "downs" be a teaching experience along the way. We may have not arrived yet; but I can say we are much closer than we were yesterday. We've come too far to turn back now.

SUCCESS WITH GOD'S WORD 32

I was inspired by a story I heard on Tennessee Crossroads of a man who had a successful BBQ restaurant for many years. When this man was about to retire; the younger man taking over the business asked him to show him the "ropes" for running the business successfully. After several suggestions, the owner reached over and picked up a Bible off a nearby shelf. He looked at the young man and said "you can't make it without this". If we want our walk with Christ to be successful we must realize how important the Bible is. The Bible is our daily bread to success; and our roadmap to Heaven.

THE POWER OF PRAYER 33

When I was young I had whooping cough and was very sick. My dad built a shed behind our house and went in there often to pray for my healing. My sisters would be outside playing and could hear him inside praying for me. James 5:16 says "the effectual fervent prayer of a righteous man availeth much". I was raised to believe that prayer changes things; and that miracles happen when a person of faith believes. Over the years I have reached out to God in prayer in situations I didn't know what to do. It was God that brought forth the answer. Prayer is the "key to Heaven; but faith unlocks the door".

RECOGNIZING JESUS 34

My former pastor from years ago would sing a hymn written by Fannie Crosby who was blind. A gentleman asked her "Fannie, do you think you will recognize Jesus when you get to heaven?" Her reply was "Oh yes I will recognize Him". This inspired her to write the song "My Savior First Of All" . The words say "I shall know Him, I shall know Him…by the prints of the nails in His hands." Well, I've never seen Him nor His hands; but I have felt the touch of His hands many times upon my life. That day when He takes my hand to welcome me to Heaven, I know I will recognize His touch because I have felt it so many times before.

A NEW LIFE-A NEW DAY 35

Each day of our life is so valuable. It's a gift from God. Today is a new day; a day God has given to each of us to live to the fullest for Him. Each of us are valuable regardless of our age or where we came from. A caterpillar perceives that it is all over… so he stays inside his cocoon. But the day comes when it's time to come out of his hiding. When he leaves the cocoon behind; he becomes a beautiful butterfly. This signifies a new life and a new beginning. The same with us. Remember, yesterday is a memory; tomorrow is a mystery; but today-the present-is a gift from God. Open your gift wisely.

OUR GOD MULTIPLIES

Every day we should start our prayer with thanking God for just being God...the Great I Am ...our help in time of trouble...our provider and on and on. If we aren't careful we will get "caught up" in the cares of this life; and overlook all the blessings. I could never stop thanking Him for all His protection and blessings He has given to us. Psalms 68:19 says "blessed be the Lord who loadeth us with benefits". The enemy comes to steal, kill and destroy; but God has come to give us life and give it more abundantly. So remember the enemy subtracts and divides; but God adds and multiplies. What an awesome God!

BRING IT ON

When my dad's mom and dad passed away, my dad took over his dad's crops. One day in the field he got real sick and got pneumonia. My dad was taught to trust God for everything. The devil told him he was going to kill him; but my dad, a man of faith, said "bring it on". After that he started improving. God had a plan for my dad's life. He had my mom reserved for him; and three daughters in the future. The enemy would like to destroy us all; but it's good to know if God be for us, who can be against us. Those are words we can depend on.

WELCOME TO THE FAMILY

Mike and I take our little Maltese to the park to ride around and look for other doggies. She gets so excited and will bark at the big ones; but stares at the small ones. She is our little rescue dog. A friend of ours found her roaming near a busy street.

She was a mess when we got her. We gave her a bath and a lot of tender-loving care; and let her know she was loved and our home was now her home. I know she is so grateful. Each of us have been rescued by God. He took us in; cleaned us up and said "welcome to the family." Finally we felt safe and secure. That's what is called unconditional love.

READY TO FLY 39

The eagle is all about taking care of her babies in the nest. The time comes when it's time to teach them to fly by getting them out of their "comfort zone". She puts twigs and sticks in the nest to make it uncomfortable. The little ones don't understand why their mother is doing this. Her desire is to teach them to fly above the clouds. In life it seems all is good; but then we feel some "pricks and bumps" along the way that are not pleasant. Ouch! It hurts. As long as we stay in the nest-we don't see what great adventures God has for us. But get ready, because God is getting us ready to fly.

THE SUPER-NATURAL 40

My husband and I have been praying for a bus for our widows. We really don't have the funds to buy this; but my husband reminds me we don't live in the natural…but the super-natural. We may not see it now; but that doesn't mean it's not coming. None of us have "super powers" but God does. What we can't do-He can. We can't do the impossible; but God specializes in the impossible situations. I believe God takes great pleasure in surprising and blessing His children. Luke 18:27 says "the things which are impossible with men are possible with God." We've learned to look for it; even if we don't see it now.

YOU ARE MY HEART'S DESIRE 41

I heard a gentle rain falling outside that brought such a peaceful sound. A thought came to my mind reminding me that's how the Holy Spirit comes to us…just when we need it most. As the rain also brings the much needed moisture needed for the crops and soil; the Holy Spirit is necessary in our daily walk with the Lord. "As the deer pants for the water, so my soul longs for you. You alone are my heart's desire and I long to worship you". Lord, may we all experience the rain of your Holy Spirit-as we walk in your presence daily and may we never be satisfied with anything less.

HIS PLANS ARE BEST 42

God knows how to handle every situation in our life. Often times we feel we know what's best and we want to be in control of it all. A young boy and his dad were sitting under a big oak tree talking. The young boy asked his dad "why did God put little walnuts on this huge big tree; and those big pumpkins on those small vines? That doesn't make sense to me". About that time a walnut fell and hit the young boy on his head. The dad replied "aren't you glad that wasn't a pumpkin?" God knows the plans He has for us; and they are perfect. All we have to do is trust Him.

GOOD ADVICE 43

I saw a sign that read "Free Advice…Good or Bad". A lot of people are out there ready to give advice whether we want it or not. Have you noticed many people will ask the advice of others when they are facing a situation and not sure what to do? I've found out God gives the best advice thru His Word. There was a sign that read "God is the answer". Under it someone else wrote "What is the question?" Under that someone wrote "It doesn't matter". That tells me God has the best answer for all of your questions. I encourage you to get His advice first when you are in doubt.

CAREFUL WHAT WE SPEAK 44

Psalms 19:4 says "Let the words of my mouth and the meditation of my heart be acceptable in thy sight O Lord". Every word we speak should be spoken carefully. My mom told me to think before I speak any words. Once they are spoken you can't take them back. The saying "your word is your bond" is so true. We can speak blessings or harm upon others. A professor gave a student a tube of toothpaste. "Squeeze all the toothpaste out into this bowl." The student did as he was told. "Now put all the toothpaste back in the tube" he told the student. "I can't do that" the student said. "Neither can words spoken against someone be taken back".

THE ROCK 45

Years ago people painted rocks with the date, city and state on the back of the rock. The rocks were placed in parks, trails, businesses or any place they could be found; so they could be picked up and placed somewhere else. The rocks may be hidden in one city and found; then placed in another city or state. Psalms 18:2 reads "the Lord is my rock...in whom will I trust". A song I like says "this rock is Jesus, yes, He's the one. This rock is Jesus, the only one. Be very sure…be very sure. Your anchor holds and grips the solid rock". Let's plant this "rock" everywhere we go.

SEEING IS BELIEVING 46

Hebrews 11:1 says "now faith is the substance of things hoped for; the evidence of things not seen." Faith holds the key to our expectations. I encourage you to make a list of things you are hoping for and a list of things you have not seen. Now believe you will see it come to pass. That is called faith. As you see those things come to pass, mark them off your list. We must always make sure the things we want lines up to the "will of God". Remember "faith is risking it all for something unseen". Most people say "I will believe it when I see it". The truth is "you will see it when you believe it".

GET CLOSER 47

I enjoy connecting with friends and family thru this "Thought For Today" daily. My husband and I have made a point to become closer to each other; but most of all to have intimate times with the Lord. It's when we spend more time with the Lord-thru prayer and Bible study-that we get to know Him better. It's also important that we have our quiet time with Him every day. I really believe God wants to speak to us daily; but the only way He can, is when we are willing to "be still and know that God is God". It is when we draw close to Him we will hear His voice. He said "draw nigh to me and I will draw nigh to you".

OUT OF THIS WORLD

We all enjoy going on vacation to just "get away".
A change of scenery does us all good. It helps us to think about the more important things in life. But vacations are temporary; and when it's time to come home, there are mixed feelings. Some people want to stay longer; but others are anxious to get home. There are places I would love to see that I have not seen. There's one place I have heard about and would love to go. People that go there find so much joy and never leave. It's like a big party with the best "host" ever. I've already got reservations to go. They call this place Heaven. It will be trip out of this world. Get your one-way ticket today.

$$\longleftrightarrow$$

THE LINE IS NEVER BUSY

When my husband lived in Missouri as a young boy; he said there was no "dial" on the phone. You would speak to the central operator and tell her who you wanted to speak to. His family's phone number was 31. The operator knew everyone. A lot has changed over the years. But calling on Jesus has never changed. Jeremiah 33:3 says "call unto me and I will answer thee". No busy signals; no operator to deal with; no call on hold either. A straight line to Heaven. Another good thing is He's available 24-7. "Central's never busy; always on the line…it's a royal service, free for one and all. When you get in trouble, give this royal line a call".

DESIRE THE MILK OF THE WORD 50

While driving thru the park, we love to watch the geese and goslings. Every time we go the babies have grown so much. They are becoming more independent by finding their own food; yet staying close to their mom for safety. When we get saved we are not to stay babies and immature. My husband years ago did a deep study of the Word. God led him to 1 Peter 2:2 "as newborn babes desire the sincere milk of the word that ye may grow thereby." If we aren't growing in the Lord, then we may not be healthy in our walk with Him. It would pay each of us to take an inventory of our growth in the Lord.

PART OF THE TEAM 51

In sports, teams are picked for each side. There are people that may not be as strong as others and may even be chosen last for a team. 1 Corinthians 1:27 tells how God "uses the weak things to confound things that are mighty." Christians feel inadequate to do great or mighty things for God. Maybe at times you feel that way; but we are all valuable to the Kingdom of God. God sees in us what we don't see. Each of us are a part of God's team; and you may hold the key needed to fulfilling the ministry. T.E.A.M... "Together Each Accomplishes Much". It's all about working together.

BE POSITIVE 52

I love to be around positive people. It's like a breath of fresh air. A lady went into the office where she worked and said "Good Morning" to her boss. His reply was "what's so good about it?"

Negative people can pull you down; but positive people will lift your spirits. Some people view a glass of water half-empty; while others see it as half-full. I love the quote that says "the pessimist sees difficulty in every opportunity; but the optimistic sees opportunity in every difficulty". Today let's be the one who is positive in our words; thoughts and actions. It will make a difference in the lives of others.

UNLOAD YOUR BURDEN 53

I was reminded of a story of a man walking home from the store with a 25lb bag of flour over his shoulder. A neighbor stopped to give the man a ride. The man was so happy to jump in because he was tired and weary. Riding home the driver noticed that his passenger was sitting in the seat with the bag of flour still over his shoulder. "Sit your load down friend. No need to carry it when you can rest". That sounds like a lot of Christians today. They carry worries; burdens; stress and cares of this life, when Jesus has told us to "cast our cares on Him".

DON'T FIX IT IF IT'S NOT BROKEN 54

Malachi 3:6 says "I am the Lord, I change not". Some changes are good; yet some are not. People are always wanting to change things such as their house; job; hairstyle or even a new mate. The saying "the grass may be greener on the other side; but when you get there, you will still have to mow it" is so true. I heard another saying years ago that read "if it's not broken, don't try to fix it". Life is full of changes; but we must accept what's available to us and make something good out of it. I'm thankful for the fact that God never changes.

THE BENEFIT PACKAGE

55

Many jobs come with benefit packages. Some come with great pay; health insurance and vacation days. As Christians we received a great benefit package when we got saved. The sad thing is many of those benefits aren't used by the Child of God. It reminds me of a couple who took a cruise and ate only cheese and crackers the entire time. When they were about to leave the ship, the Caption of the ship asked them why they didn't eat from the buffet. Their reply was "they couldn't afford it"; not realizing it came with the price of the cruise. Enjoy God's buffet daily. It was paid "in full" thousands of years ago.

WE WIN!

56

A young boy was running in a race and so excited. He could hear his dad cheering him on in the crowd. The young boy tripped and fell, but got back up again. Down the road he tripped again; but got up again and went to the finish line-coming in fifth place. The young boy was so discouraged. His dad grabbed him and said "I am so proud of you. To me you won. When you fell, you got back up-both times." That's how God feels when we fall and get back up. Just because we have fallen a few times doesn't mean we aren't winning this race. Just remember failure isn't final with the Lord.

SHOWING LOVE

57

Luke 6:31 says "as ye would that men should do to you, do ye also to them". That simply says for us to treat people like we want to be treated. Many people have been wounded by words or actions of others. It's hard to heal that injury. But you and I can make a big difference in the lives of others; and help bring healing to them. This saying is so true. "I've learned people will forget what you said; what you did in life; but never forget how you made them feel". You and I can make a great impression on others by showing God's love. That's the best healing agent.

BIGGER THAN THE MOON   58

Years ago people would ask for a moon-pie and a cold RC drink. I read where a salesman asked the coal miners when they were on break if they wanted a snack. One of the miners on break asked for a graham cracker and a marshmallow "as big as the moon". That inspired the moon pie to come about. Often times as Christians we hesitate to ask God for big things we need in our life. But we serve a big God and it is His pleasure to fulfill the needs of His children. The next time you need something from God…think big; ask big; and believe big… bigger than the moon!

DON'T QUIT!   59

My sister in school had to memorize a long poem entitled "Don't Quit". It says "Life is strange with its twists and turns; as everyone of us sometimes learns. And many a failure comes about-when he might have won had he stuck it out." Sometimes life seems crazy; but we must hold tight, don't give up and win this battle. The battle is not ours anyway, says the Lord. The poem goes on to say "when you are hardest hit; when things seem worst-you must not quit". If we just hold fast, we will win this battle. So I encourage each of us to don't give up or quit. Let's stick it out. We are almost home.

THE SMALL STUFF 60

We've heard the saying "don't sweat the small stuff". It's the little things that can really bug us. As my sister and I were walking one day, I felt something in my shoe that really hurt. When I took my shoe off, it was just a small pebble...but it felt like a rock every time I took a step. If we aren't careful we can allow little things to get in our way of doing what God intended us to do. Those little things can grow into big things if we aren't careful. Enjoy life. We only pass this way once. Don't let the little things hinder the blessings God intended for you today.

THE TRAINING WHEELS 61

When I was a child my dad put training wheels on my bike to keep me from falling off. The day came when my dad took the training wheels off-encouraging me to ride on my own. I do remember my dad going beside me to make me feel safe; but it was rather scary. I feel as Christians it's time for us to take the "training wheels" off and focus ahead and move forward. It's then we lean entirely upon the Lord. Just remember, "life should not be a journey where we arrive in a pretty, preserved body; but maybe skidding in sideways; worn out and shouting Wow! What a ride!!"

WELL DONE-MISSION ACCOMPLISHED 62

My dad loved working at Dunbar Cave! I was born in a cabin on the property of that park. I was very quiet growing up; but I always enjoyed life. I accepted the Lord when I was a teen right after my dad passed away. It amazes me how God chose a country girl to be in ministry for Him. We are all born for a purpose in life. God has a mission for us to fulfill. Our missions are all different; but it's up to us to do the best we can; and hear His words "well done my child". I urge you to find what God Has chosen you to do; and do it with all your might. God doesn't call the qualified but qualifies those He calls.

THE BEAUTY OF IT ALL   63

There are a lot of things in life we can see beauty in. The laughter of a child; a perfect rose; or a rainbow in the sky. I always see beauty in the face of a saint of God; the years expressed on the face of a vet; or even a widow or orphan. But the greatest beauty is the Love of God reaching a sinner in the lowest pit. The beauty is found in our Heavenly Father who sent His only begotten son that you and I could be saved. These are things that bring out the real beauty; and no make-up is needed. Psalms 27:4 "one thing I have desired of the Lord, that will I seek after…to behold the beauty of the Lord, and to inquire in His temple".

THE FLIGHT OF THE GEESE   64

I continue to enjoy driving thru the park and watching the geese. It's amazing how geese know to fly south for the winter. I've watched them many times as they fly in a "V" formation. They take turns in the front; moving to the back when they are tired. They say those that fly alone-beat their wings more frequently and have higher heart rates. We as Christians should follow this example. No child of God should struggle alone. When we become a team-no one becomes worn-out; weary; or burned out. Just remember-you aren't alone. We will make this flight together.

THE MASTER PIECE   65

I've watched the potter hold a piece of clay that appeared to be a waste. The potter takes that piece of clay, works with it and removes any unwanted sticks or rocks. It was a process; but finally it's time for him to put it into the fire. The heat does wonders for that piece of "work". When he completes his piece of art, he proudly displays his "master-piece". At one time we were like that piece of clay-nothing to brag about. But when God picked us up and began his process; we became a piece of work that He was proud of. He called it "His Master-piece". "As the clay is in the potter's hand; so are you in my hands". Jeremiah 18:5.

BEAR ONE ANOTHER'S BURDENS   66

Many people have gone thru difficult times in their life. The Bible says "bear ye one another's burdens". We must be sensitive to the Holy Spirit. Don't hesitate to pray for someone God lays on your heart. "Lord help us not to just say 'we care' or 'we are praying for you' without acting on the words we speak." Pick up the phone and call that person God lays on your heart. Our voice can be His voice; our hands can be His hands and our compassion can represent His Love. Let's help bear one another's burdens. Someone is needing you and me to reach out to them today.

HIS RESOURCES-NOT LIMITED

Years ago we went to Beech Bend Park and walked around to feed the animals. When we came to the Ape's cage, the ape knocked the channel down. My husband was just about to feed him. We went on to the other animals and came back by the ape's cage. The ape was holding his hands "cupped" under the channel he had put back up. My husband thought "how stupid-I wanted to feed you earlier-but you wouldn't let me". God spoke to my husband-reminding him he had done the same thing when He had wanted to bless him. Just remember, God doesn't limit His resources. Keep the channel open.

←——————————————→

YOUR HAND IN HIS

You may recall a song made popular years ago titled "Put Your Hand In The Hand". Growing up I always felt secure when I had my hand in my dad's hand in a crowd of people. Many times He would reach out and grab my hand to let me know he was right there and I had nothing to fear. A lot of times in life, things can seem big, scary and overwhelming. If we can remind ourselves to put our hand in God's hand; things can become calm and peaceful. When His hand touches our hand, things begin to change and our outlook looks different and brighter. Today "put your hand in the hand of the man who stilled the waters".

←——————————————→

SET THE GLASS DOWN

A teacher walked across the classroom holding a glass of water. "How heavy is this glass of water?" she asked. Her students shouted out different answers across the room. "It depends on how long you hold it" she replied. "The longer I hold it, the more strain it puts on my arm" she said. Once I set the glass down, the weight is lifted. It is important that we lay down every weight, burden or care we are carrying. Jesus said "cast all your cares on Him-for He cares for you." If you are still feeling the weight of the world, give it to Jesus. It's time we set the "glass" and "stress" down.

NOT EASILY BROKEN 70

A father had two sons who argued all the time. The dad gave each boy a bundle of sticks. He told both of his sons to take each bundle apart and then break each stick. The one that finished first was the winner. Next he gave a bundle of sticks to each boy again, and told them to not take the bundles apart, but break the bundle into pieces. The boys came back saying they were unable to do it. The dad looked at his sons and said "boys remember this lesson. We are much stronger when we all work together rather than alone". It's important we "pull together not apart". Ecclesiastes 4:12 says "a threefold cord isn't quickly broken."

WELCOME HOME 71

My husband and I go visit a church that honors the motorcycle community every year. I've stood on their porch with the members of that church and watched for the group to come and turn into the parking lot. You can hear them coming from a great distance away. As they turn in, the people start cheering and clapping as if to say "Welcome. We are here to cheer you home". I feel that will be the way it is when we get to Heaven. The saints will be shouting and clapping as we walk thru the portals of Glory. We can hear the same words "welcome home"! What a blessed thought and what a great home-coming that will be.

SOMETHING NEW 72

A man's daughter was going thru a tough time. The dad put three pots of boiling water on the stove. One had potatoes; another one had eggs; and the last one had a cinnamon teabag in it. He asked the daughter what she saw. She told him each item in each pot. The dad said "That's right. The potatoes have become soft. If you take the shell off of the egg-its a hardboiled egg. The taste and smell of the tea will bring a smile to your face. They all faced the same adversity; but the teabag changed the water creating something new. When facing hot water which will we be?

ALL THINGS ARE POSSIBLE 73

I read of an older man who was broke; living in a tiny house and driving a beat-up car. This man was living on $99.00 social security each month. He was encouraged by others to share his chicken recipe in restaurants; but I read where he was rejected 1009 times before he got a "yes". Col. Sanders changed the way Americans eat chicken. God has given each of us dreams; visions and goals; but not everyone will "catch" our vision. I encourage you to hold to it tightly. Habakkuk 2:3 says "for the vision is yet for an appointed time.....though it tarries; wait for it." Because with God "all things are possible".

TAKE THE CHALLENGE 74

There is a lot of challenges we face in life. I remember my husband teaching me to drive a 5-speed car. It was a challenge; but I learned I could do it if I would just put my mind to it. I also remember him teaching me to drive in the snow. He took me to the bottom of a steep hill and told me to put it in 4-wheel drive. It was a little scary; but he assured me I could do it. After I learned the ropes; it was so exciting. With each challenge we face, we can conquer all our fears. Face each challenge with your "faith-on" because I know you and I can do it! Remove all doubt and step out by faith.

A TREASURE TO GOD 75

A speaker was speaking to a crowd of about 200 people. He held up a twenty dollar bill and asked who would like to have it. Two hundred hands went up. He crumpled the bill and again he asked who wanted it. All hands went up again. He dropped the bill on the floor and stomped on it asking who would still want it if he gave it away. Again all hands went up. He made a remark that was so interesting. "Regardless of what I did to this bill; it did not lose its value'. Friend regardless of what we've encountered or been thru in life; we are still of great value and a treasure to God.
Nothing can change that.

TIME: USE WISELY 76

Let's suppose we had a bank account that put $86,400.00 in our account every day. If we didn't use it each day we would lose it. I'm sure we would withdraw every penny of it daily making sure we got it all. We all have an account we call TIME. It credits us 86,400.00 seconds every day. We can't carry over time from this day until tomorrow. We must ask ourselves a question every day. "Did I use my time wisely; or did I waste any time God gave me; or did I share my time with others"? Time is very valuable. Count every minute and use it wisely.

THE GIFT 77

My husband and I realize the money we have is not ours. The Scripture says all "the silver and gold is His". It is our job to be good stewards of the money God has given to us. I love the quote "the meaning of life is to find your gift. The purpose of life is to give it away". This doesn't mean just money; but our talents; our love and our prayers make great gifts to give away. Often-times when we share our gifts with others in their need; our own needs are met also. We cannot out give God. It will come back "good measure, pressed down and running over". Luke 6:38. Cast your bread upon the waters, for you shall find it after many days. Ecclesiastes 11:2

LIVE TODAY TO THE FULLEST 78

When I come to the end of this journey I only want people to say "she made a difference in the lives of others". At the cemetery we see two dates on the head-stone. The day the person was born and the day they passed away. The only thing that matters is the "dash" in the middle of those two dates. That indicates what the person accomplished in their lifetime and what accomplishments they made. At the close of our life

it's not the years in our life; but the life in our years that really matters. We must live today as if it was our last.
None of us have the promise of tomorrow.

BE A DAD TO REMEMBER

79

My husband got his dad a plaque that read "Anyone can be a father; but it takes someone special to be a dad". I think about people that fit this quote so well. My dad was number one in my book. He not only lived the life; but taught us how to live this life. My dad was the example for us to know how to pray and believe God. My dad passed away when I was fifteen. I felt like I had lost my best friend; but my pastor stepped up and became a "father-figure" to me. He was there when I needed him most. Most of all, I'm thankful for God that became my heavenly father. God is aware of what we need.

A BLESSED BASKET

80

I remember my dad planting seeds in our garden. It was exciting to watch those vegetables begin to grow. My dad never planted tomatoes expecting to find squash; or cucumbers to find carrots. What are we sowing today? If we sow discord we can't expect there to be harmony. At the same time we can't sow doubt and expect to have faith. The Bible says "what we sow that shall we also reap". My niece is always bringing a basket of goodies filled with so much love. Our basket can be used to bless and share with others. Let's sow joy, peace and God's love with others. Let's be a "blessing basket" along this journey.

ICE CREAM CHALLENGE 81

A friend told me she could live on Ice Cream. Of all the flavors you could choose, I never understood why a person would choose plain vanilla. You can get an old-fashioned banana split with 3 flavors of ice cream; with a banana and toppings; coolwhip; nuts and cherry. Just looking at it will make your mouth water. If you leave the banana out, it will not be a banana split. It will be more like a sundae. The same with us. We can't become a Christian without Jesus. He makes it complete. If you ask me, that's much better than ice cream; and you can live on it the rest of your life.

FEEL FOR THE TUG 82

I remember going fishing with my dad. We would throw our lines out in the water and wait patiently for a bite. I can still remember when I would feel a "tug" on my line. That meant a fish was biting or may even be caught on the line. I learned to bait my hook and even take the fish off the hook. But my dad would clean our fish…that was his job. The same with us. We can lead a person to the Lord; but it is up to God to clean that person up. As a Christian we should be ready to lead someone to the Lord every opportunity we get. Who knows, someone may be waiting for the "tug" you and I can give to lead them to the Lord.

THE LIGHT IS THERE 83

Living in the City you can't see many things. Growing up in the country on a dark night; looking up in the sky I could see the stars and moon clearly. I would watch for "lightening bugs" to come my way. In the city you take for granted they are all there. In our life when there's not a cloud in our life we see clearly; and we have a tendency to forget God is there. But in our darkest day we look up and His love is shining down on us, even if we don't see Him. The song says "the God of the day is still God in the night". 1John 1:5 says "God is light and in Him is no darkness at all". Look for Him in your darkest moment. He will be there.

OH WHAT A SAVIOR 84

When I gave my heart to the Lord; it was the best decision I ever made. It filled a vacancy in my life. If there's something missing in your life; take this step found in Romans. "We have all sinned and come short of the Glory of God. If we confess our sins….He will forgive us of all our sins". Pray this prayer: "Jesus I come to you just as I am. I confess my sins and ask you to forgive me. I know you died on the cross for me. Thank you for forgiving me and coming into my heart. From this day forth I will live for you to the best of my ability". And our Savior will do just that.

SWEETER AND SWEETER 85

As a little girl, I remember how exciting it was to go into a store and get to choose a candy bar. The problem was there were so many to choose from, I didn't know which one I wanted. Like the candy bars Jesus has a variety of blessings He has available for each of us. He gives us "Mounds" of joy; a "Bit-of-Honey" along the way; thinking about it makes me want to "Snicker".

I never want to "Take-5" but I always want "S'mores". This Christian life is worth a "100 Grand". One day we will have a great "Pay-Day" and we will pass the "Milky Way". It gets sweeter and sweeter as the days go by.

THE BEST PART OF YOUR DAY 86

I was thinking of the commercial "the best part of waking up is Folgers in your cup". Many will say "I have to have my cup of coffee before I get going". In fact they won't be in a good mood if they don't get that cup of coffee. It's so great to wake up in the morning knowing Jesus is there and will go with us every step of the way. I believe we should wake up each day and say "Good Morning Lord" and ask for His guidance during the day. He makes everyday so much better. With Him we can go thru anything. Just remember "the best part of waking up is Jesus in your heart".

THE SPECIALIST 87

Often times when things go wrong, we try to "fix-it" without asking for help. It's like putting something together without reading the instructions; or getting lost and not asking for directions. In our day-to-day walk, Jesus wants us to ask for His directions for that day. I've heard people say "I've tried everything, all I know to do now is try God". I've never understood that. I think God wants us to seek Him first. That would save us a lot of time and money. The Bible says to "seek Him first and all these other things will be added". He is the master specialist and there is absolutely "nothing He can't do".

CELEBRATING TWO BIRTHDAYS 88

Each of us were born on a certain day of the month. When that day comes around we call it our birthday. Kids love to celebrate this day with a party, balloons, cake and gifts. Yet many adults don't care to celebrate their birthday. I for one think every birthday is special because it is a day the Lord has given to us; and another year He has brought us thru. There's another birthday we should celebrate, The day we gave our heart to the Lord and became a child of the King. It's not just "another day" but a day that changed our life. I encourage you to celebrate both birthdays!

THE BOOM-BOOMS 89

Firecrackers; fireworks or gunshots are so terrifying to our little dog. She becomes nervous and wants my husband to hold her every time she hears a boom-boom. We can sense her nervousness and feel her shaking. I think she feels safe with him and knows he won't let anything hurt her. When life brings some frightful moments; it's then we run to Jesus, our shelter. We are protected and in "good hands" with our Savior. I love Psalms 91:1 "thou shalt not be afraid for the terror by night." V10 "there shall no evil befall thee, neither shall any plague come nigh thy dwelling". Friend don't let the "boom booms" of life terrify you. Run to Jesus!

A TUNE-UP 90

After a certain amount of miles we must take our vehicle in for a tune-up. If it is not taken care of, more serious problems can arise; costing a lot more money. Maybe it would be good if we took an inventory of our life. We could use a tune-up on our plans; attitude; thought-life; life-style and our priorities. Christ can handle any situation we may have. We must do this regularly and apply Psalms 51 to our life. "Create in me a clean heart O God and renew a right spirit within me". That's a good tune-up and no appointment is needed for it. And there's no charge.

THANK GOD FOR FREEDOM 91

I have great memories of 4th of July's at the Cave near our home where my dad worked. The food, paddle-boats; sky-diving and fireworks were so amazing to me. Later in years I enjoyed the 4th with our nieces at a park; picnics or even lunch at home. Independence Day is the day we celebrate our country; its freedom; and for those who sacrificed their life so we could enjoy this freedom. But I will never forget the man Jesus who died on the cross for our freedom from sin. If you ask me that's the best freedom we could ever experience. "Where the spirit of the Lord is, there is freedom" and "For whom the spirit sets free is free indeed".

SATISFACTION GUARANTEED 92

My husband and I decided to create a stir-fry dish that was delicious. I cut up the vegetables and Mike added the meat and seasoning. We cooked it slow in our electric skillet. It was a great meal I'm sure we will use over and over. That's the way it is with our walk with the Lord. It never gets old; but He sends us "new" blessings everyday for us to enjoy. It's like He puts all the spices of life together and mixes it with His love to bring a satisfaction to us. It's true "only Jesus can satisfy your soul… He'll give you peace you never knew-sweet joy and love and Heaven too".

←——————————→

YOU CAN WEATHER THE STORM   93

We have a friend who is a great inspiration to us. He's talented; and been used by the Lord in many ways. He sings; plays the piano; and has directed choirs over the years. We've watched him walk thru some difficult times in his life. He has risen above every heartache; every storm and been determined to live his life to the fullest for Christ. The road hasn't been easy; but he has proven we can weather any storm when we have Christ on our side. Friend each of us can make it because we aren't walking this road alone. Christ is always with us.
He will help us over every obstacle to a peaceful landing.

←——————————→

HIGH PRIORITY   94

We hear about things that are essential in our life. Along with that we also hear the words "high priority". In this life we need to walk close to our Savior. We need to remove "fake" mask and "be real". We must be positive in our faith for the Lord and keep our distance from fear and doubt. We must always be "open" to the Holy Spirit and what He has for each of us daily. If we follow these guidelines; we will experience a fuller and enlightening walk with God; and our walk with Him will be safe and rewarding. We need to make sure our priorities are in line.

ACTIONS AND WORDS

95

"Birds of a feather flock together". It's amazing how geese stay together and keep watch for the enemy ahead. They make sure they watch out for the others around them. As Christians we need each other. We must "stick together" watching for danger ahead. Never harbor ill feelings against others. People are watching to see how we will react to situations we encounter in life. The saying "actions speak louder than words" is so true. Are we willing to go the extra mile to make things right? If we have a forgiving heart; then we too will be forgiven.

HE IS OUR GUIDE

96

My dad gave tours while working at a local cave years ago. One day he had a group in the back of the cave when the lights went out. My dad, with a flashlight, asked each person to put their hand on the shoulder of the person in front of them and follow him thru the darkness. Safely He brought the group out. In life we are faced with dark moments in our life. In those moments we need to remember who our guide is. Just as my dad, our Lord is familiar with the journey and knows the way out of the darkness. We must keep our hand in His; and follow Him, for He is our light and our guide.

RIGHT WHERE YOU ARE

97

I watched our General Overseer preach a message that touched my heart. The message was "What We Must Not Lose". He said we must not lose our foundation; our faith; our fire, or our zeal. If we lose any of these, our walk with God becomes a chore and we will become "burned out" right where we are. In every season of your life, prepare to spend more time with God and get to know Him better. Spend more time in prayer and in the Word of God. This always draws us closer to Him. I can guarantee you, He will meet you right where you are.

EXPIRATION DATE 98

A lot of times things we buy will show an expiration date on them if we look. Our lives are like that. We all have an expiration date; but none of us know when it is. The Bible says our days are all numbered. I am glad there are some things that do not carry an expiration date on them. For instance the day I got saved the salvation plan did not say "good only to a certain day". If we stay close to Him and away from sin, our salvation is good until eternity. His love-joy-peace and mercy never expires either. Think about it. Aren't we glad His grace is sufficient until the end without expiring.

DON'T ANSWER 99

My husband and I are so tired of "robo" calls. My husband was on the phone with a lady trying to sell him something. He kept saying "no thanks… I'm not interested….not today. No I don't want it". Finally my husband said "wait a minute, listen what is it about NO you don't understand?" That's the way the enemy works with us. He will not give up. He will keep trying and trying. We must show him who he's dealing with and whose child we are. Let him know we will not accept his lies and our ears are not garbage cans. Remind him we are refusing to answer his calls. So he might as well leave.

TRUST HIS HEART

100

During tough times in our life, we can experience the greatest moments with God. We can sense His love and power in a greater way. It's during these times we should ask God for His wisdom and His guidance. It's during these times He may be wanting to teach us something. We never know what God has in store for each of us; but one thing I do know is God walks with us thru it all. "Some thru the waters; some thru the fire… God leads His dear children along". Friend when you feel uncertain and you don't know what God is doing in your life; and you don't see His hand….Friend just trust His heart

FOLLOW THE LEADER

101

We were driving thru the park when one of the geese decided to cross in front of us. He was going at a very "slow pace" taking his time. As he was crossing, other geese decided they were going to follow him, holding up the traffic. As a child we played a game called "follow the leader". There would be one in the lead, while the rest of us followed where he went and did what he did. I urge each of us to follow our leader-Jesus. He knows where He is taking us and He will not lead us astray. When we follow Him, it is a guarantee we will cross over to the other side and make it to our destination.

HE FIGHTS FOR US

102

Isaiah 54:17 says "no weapon formed against us shall prosper". When someone or anything comes against us, they are coming against God, because we are His children. He said He is our

"refuge and strength, a very present help in time of trouble".
I always remember the story of David. God reminded him
that He would be with him in the battle. And we read how
He helped him win the battle. Friend "the battle is not ours
but God's". Don't give up on the fight...remember you are not
fighting alone, because He will fight for us. If God be for us,
who can be against us anyway. And sure enough, the victory
will be ours.

HOME-RUN 103

Baseball teams have a coach to help direct their movements.
The coach may seem "harsh" at times; but it is for their good,
because he wants them to win. Our coach Jesus will spend
every moment with us to make sure we go the right direction
and make the right choices. He wants each of us to be on the
"winning team". He doesn't want us to "foul out" or "strike out".
He is so proud we are on His team. If we listen to Him, we will
win! And each of us will make a home-run. We won't be sliding
in to base; but running and shouting all the way.

RUN TO THE SHEPHERD 104

I love the story of the shepherd in the Bible who goes out to find
the one lost sheep. He searches until he finds it; and brings it
safely home. Maybe you or someone you know is straying from
the fold. Our shepherd, Jesus will go the extra mile to bring you
or that person back home. He will never give up. The prodigal
son finally "came to himself" and decided to go home. It was
then he ran to his father, even though he didn't feel worthy to be
his son. His cry was "father forgive me". My friend, I encourage

you to run to the shepherd. His arms are open wide to embrace you.

———————————————→

TIME SNEAKS UPON US   105

It's amazing how things can sneak up on us. For example: Time. A child thinks it takes forever for his birthday to get here; but we adults think ours come around quickly. James 4:14 says "what is your life...a vapour that appeareth for a little while and vanisheth away". We have good intentions of doing things; but put them off because we can do it "tomorrow". But they never get done. Think about it? Is there something God wants us to do like making things right with someone? Do we need to pick up some broken pieces or dreams and get it done? Don't put off for tomorrow what can be done today.

———————————————→

WHAT DO THEY SEE?   106

I love food that has been grilled. A lot of times you can go out into the yard and smell the aroma in the air where a neighbor is grilling. There are certain things that will attract people. For example a parade; fireworks; good food and parties. As a Christian we must have the radiance of the Holy Spirit in our life that will attract others to Christ. The way we walk, talk and live must be enticing to others, that they too will want what we have. So as we walk this journey, may we not walk it alone. But may others follow us because they like what they see in us.

OUR WORLD NEEDS JESUS

People are looking for peace and love. The only way people can experience real peace is thru Jesus Christ. Everyone is needing an answer; but Christ is the only remedy and solution to all the problems in our world. We need to see a change....but the change needs to begin in our own life. When we change, we can make a difference in our family, neighbors, city and state. The answer comes when we say "Lord not my will but thine be done". We are all in need of more of Him every day we live. Yes the only answer for our world is Jesus.

ONLY A HIC-CUP

I don't know about you, but I do not like having hic-cups at all. To get rid of them I have tried water; sugar or even holding my breath. There are "hic-cups" that occur in our day-to-day living. Everything can be going real good; and then they just show up when you least expect them. They can cause frustration and even "mess up" our plans; but often times God allows these to occur to slow us down or to center our vision on Him. He just may have a better plan than ours; and the only way He can get our attention is to send them our way. So don't despise hic-cups that come your way. Look for the good through these.

HARVEST TIME

In the fall you can drive thru the country, and see farmers in the field cutting down corn-stalks, soy beans and wheat. It's there you can see big rolls of hay laying out in the fields. Most of the veggies have been picked to be canned or frozen for the winter months ahead. This is called "harvest time". Spiritually the fields are ready. Sinners are still waiting to hear the gospel. Time is running out. Friends and family need to be saved. An old song says it well: "It's harvest time-the Savior's calling; the grain is falling. O do not wait; it's getting late. Its Harvest time".

CROWN HIM KING 110

There's a board game that has been around for many years called CHECKERS involving two players. I remember playing this game when I was young. To win the game you must control the board and prepare to move forward. You must stay alert of your opponent and aim for the King's position for safer moves. The player that cannot move loses the game. In life, we must control our moves and actions daily; moving forward and never go backwards. We must aim toward the King's position-our Heavenly Father. Aim for the "far-side" to Heaven. It is then we can crown Him King.

FIND THE MISSING PIECE 111

People choose hobbies in their spare time. Our good friends had a ministry called "Helping Hands" who worked puzzles. You could walk into the building and a puzzle was always on the table ready to be completed. I enjoyed looking on the walls and seeing many completed puzzles displayed. I enjoy doing puzzles; but it can be aggravating if a piece is missing. The puzzle can never be completed. People try so many things to have their life completed. Things will not "fill in" for the piece that is missing in our life. The only thing that makes our life complete is Jesus. Don't go another step without Him.

WELL DONE CHILD

Our nieces and nephews are amazing. They check on us often. They each have goals they want to reach in their lives. We must have goals to reach regardless of our age. It's up to us to be faithful in the calling God has laid out for us. Just as many of my nieces and nephews have gotten good grades and gotten their diplomas with honors; we too will receive our "diploma" from our Savior. I know He is keeping good records on each of us regardless of what others think. The best comment on our heavenly diploma would read "Well done my child". What a graduation day that will be!

A BETTER UPGRADE

Mike and I have ordered groceries on-line many times. Sometimes when they are out of an item we ordered, they upgrade it to a better, more expensive item. I must say that's ok with me. In fact I am very satisfied. Many of us make our request known to God; but when we don't get what we ask for, we are sad and disappointed. Have you ever thought that maybe God has a better thing for you? I would call that an "up-grade". Don't be surprised if God chooses something better for you in the future; than what you asked for in the beginning. For me, that is perfectly ok.

A GREAT IMPACT

There are many teachers that have made an impact on my life. First, there are Sunday School teachers that instilled in me Godly principles. Then there are elementary and high school teachers that really made a difference in my life. They taught me many valuable lessons. My parents, sisters and former pastor were great examples in my life. I credit them for helping me to be where I am today. I've learned a lot from my husband during our marriage. He taught me the value of having compassion and love for others. But the best teacher is my Heavenly Father. He is the guide I need; and the Word is the roadmap I need to follow.

NEVER THIRST AGAIN 115

Growing up my dad and others worked long days in the hot fields. One day a worker went to the country store to get sodas for everyone. When he asked me what kind I wanted, I said "Purple" meaning grape. As a young girl I remember how good that soda tasted that hot day. In the Bible a woman came to the well to get water; and met Jesus who offered her living water. Jesus told her "whoever drinks the water I give, will never thirst again". Today you and I need that living water. Nothing in this world will satisfy or take His place. As Christians we become dry and thirsty in this cruel world. Let's drink the water that springs up from deep inside.

THE VISION IS POSSIBLE 116

Mike and I work with the seniors and widows in our community. We love to invest in the lives of these who have blazed the trails for all of us. I love the scripture Psalms 37:25 that says "I have been young and now am old; yet have I not seen the righteous forsaken, nor his seed begging bread". Our vision for this ministry is to have a place where these people can come for a few days to just "get away" with God. In the natural I'm not sure how it will come to pass; but we know the vision is possible with God. "Though the vision tarry, wait for it, it shall surely come to pass".

FATHER KNOWS BEST 117

My husband and I have a seven year old nephew that is cute as a button. He never meets a stranger. He never lets things get him down. He's "all boy" and sometimes gets in trouble and gets "time out" . Sure he will fuss and pout; but its not long before he is full of joy again. Many times you and I may encounter "time out" too. Often times we try to do things on our own; and God says "no" because He knows what is best for us. Like my nephew, we may fuss and pout but I can reassure you, our Father knows what's best for us. All we have to do is trust Him.

RESTORE THE JOY 118

I remember my first year of school. My parents got my list of books and school supplies to be picked up. We went into town and purchased those items. I was excited; but the real excitement came when I climbed on that big bus the first day of school. When I came home I could not stop talking. I wanted to tell every event of the day. When we first got saved, we wanted to tell everyone. Somehow over the years, if we aren't careful we will not have the same zeal we once had. It is imperative we ask God to restore the joy of our salvation so others will desire this walk with Jesus. It can be Joy unspeakable and full of joy.

COME JUST AS YOU ARE

I love the words to the old hymn "Just As I Am". That song says we don't have to impress anyone; or try to be someone we aren't when we come to Jesus. All He wants is for us to come to him as we are; whether we are broken, depressed, despondent or hurt. It doesn't matter if we are rich or poor; He will be standing there with His arms open wide and saying "welcome home child". None of us are "too bad" or "too poor" or "too broken" to come to Him. He can "fix" anything wrong in our life. Friend if you really want a friend…come to Jesus. He loves you just as you are; and He will never turn you away.

$$\longleftrightarrow$$

A TOTAL COMMITMENT

120

I heard a cute story about a chicken and a pig traveling together. As they entered a small town they saw a sign that read "Fresh eggs and Ham". The chicken said "let's go in". The pig was reluctant. "I don't think so" he said. The chicken said "why not"? The pig said "if they see us they may want to use us for breakfast. For you it would be just a contribution; but for me it would be a total commitment". Sometimes we just want to make a contribution of our life to Christ; but friend God's looking for a total commitment. He wants one hundred percent; ninety nine just won't do.

$$\longleftrightarrow$$

OUT OF THE SHELL

121

My mom used to make fresh coconut cakes. She would buy a fresh coconut; remove the shell and grate the coconut. She used the coconut milk to soak into the cake to make it moist.

She would place the grated coconut on the outside of the cake. The finished product was awesome; my favorite. People find themselves in a shell not wanting to come out because of fear; hurt; disappointment; or lack of confidence. Like the caterpillar in the cocoon-it does not become a beautiful butterfly until it breaks out of its shell. I encourage you to discover what God has in store for you outside of the shell. He will make something beautiful of your life.

TAKE IT TO THE BANK   122

I love the hymn "Great Is Thy Faithfulness". Many people encounter unfaithfulness in their life. This results in lack of trust in people. I'm so thankful God never goes back on His Word. Even when others let us down or disappoint us; it's good to know Christ will never do that. I love the hymn that says "Tis so sweet to trust in Jesus; just to take Him at His Word; just to rest upon His promises-just to know thus saith the Lord". If you need a faithful friend-look to Jesus. He's the best friend you will ever find. He will always be faithful-and you can take that to the bank.

THE SHOE THAT FITS   123

I recall going downtown as a young girl to get new shoes. I remember being fitted for the right size. We've heard the saying "if the shoe fits; wear it". Often times we hear this after a sermon; teaching or comment is made. Sometimes people will judge others before they really know a person or what they are going thru. People handle things the best they can. We never know how we would respond to a situation until we are there.

A true saying is "don't judge a person until you've walked a mile in their shoes". We must pray "Lord help our steps to be ordered by you-so we can see others in a different perspective".

GOD'S UNCHANGING HAND 124

I remember the night my dad went to be with the Lord. That day was like all others. My dad got up and went to work; came home-ate supper and then we all gathered in the living room to have our family prayer. That night God called him home. Life and daily routines change; but God never changes. You will notice lifestyles change or the way we do things change especially since we have more modern technology. Some changes are good; and some are hard to get used to. I am so thankful Jesus is the same yesterday, today and forever. He never changes. Friend let's hold to His unchanging hand.

NO SUBSTITUTION 125

My husband found a new cake recipe for me to try. I didn't have all the ingredients so I made a few substitutions. I have to say it actually turned out good in spite of the substitutions I had to make. Sometimes we make some substitutions in life; but there are some things that cannot be substituted. For instance you can not substitute God's love or His Redemption plan. Only Jesus can save us; and forgive us. Only He can walk with us and be our best friend. There is no message-but God's-that can change our heart. Make sure you stick to the "real" message of the cross. Jesus is the "real thing".

HIS EYE IS ON US

126

Our little dog most times will not go off the porch unless I come outside with her. Her eye is always on me to see if I am coming outside with her. She loves to go and get on our picnic table and make observations in every direction. Mike calls it "her observation deck". Just as I watch her-I'm thankful we have a heavenly father who keeps close watch over us. Just as our dog watches every direction; it is needful you and I keep an eye out for the attacks of the enemy. But it is comforting to know our heavenly father is watching over you and me. Yes "His eye is on the sparrow and I know He watches me."

←————————————————→

HOME AT LAST

127

Mike and I have been blessed to travel to many states. Each state is unique in its own way. The flowers; roads; stores and buildings are different everywhere we go. But there's no place like home. We bought our home about 41 years ago. We looked at many houses; but when we saw this one we knew it was home. But this is just a temporary place for us to stay. You see "this world is not our home; we're just passing thru." What I am saying is our final destination will be Heaven. When we walk inside the gates of that city-I know we will feel welcome; and we can declare "home at last".

←————————————————→

ALL IN A NAME

128

Each of us were given a name when we were born. Some carry their mom's name; others their dads. Many people have earned even a nick-name. When a lady gets married, most will change their name to their husband's name. A name is very important. Our name should be one of integrity. We must have a "good name in standing". When others hear our name-it should be a reflection of our testimony in Christ. Our name should reflect honesty and trust. Proverbs 22:1 says "a good name is rather to be chosen than riches". Our name carries the name of Jesus-because we are His child.

THE CHANGE OF SEASONS   129

I love the four seasons; and all their attributes. I look forward to each one. I like the snow in the winter; the beauty of the spring; the summer brings on vacations; and the fall reflects the beautiful change of colors. No season is perfect. Each of us have different seasons in our life. Some are good; some not so pleasant. But God uses every season to minister to our life. Without the storms-we wouldn't appreciate the beautiful sun. Without the cold bitter days-we wouldn't enjoy the spring as much. The next time you are going thru a season in your life you really don't like; just remember-this season will change for the better.

HE WILL MEET YOU   130

I've heard the saying "we can't get there from here." We've been down roads in our travels where we were trying to find a location when I've actually felt that way. But we found the way; even if we had to ask someone for directions. If you are going down a road in life and it seems there's no way out; I want to tell you I know someone that can help you find your way. It may look impossible; but with God it's possible. If you really feel you can't get to God from where you are; I will tell you that God knows where you are and He knows His way to you.

EXPLORE THE PAGES 131

One day a preacher many years ago went to visit a family in his church. The dad looked at his son and said "Hey Johnny go get the book your mom reads all the time". The young son came back with a Sears Catalog. My mom ordered items for us girls from catalogs. We were excited when the mailman left a package in the mailbox. But these never took the place of the Bible in our home. The important things were only found in the Bible. We must never allow dust to accumulate on God's word. Friend I encourage each of us to explore the pages. We will be amazed at what we find in there. It is the best roadmap or GPS we will ever need.

COVERING A MULTITUDE OF SINS 132

Growing up my mom would wash clothes and take them outside to hang on the clothesline. I still remember watching them blow in the wind. When those clothes were brought back in, they had such a fresh-air smell. That's the way it is with God's spirit upon our life. Nothing takes the place of the sweet Holy Spirit. It is "more desired than gold; and sweeter than honey and the honeycomb". The fragrance of the Holy Spirit in our life can lift the spirit of others. The Holy Spirit is the "make-up" we need on our countenance to those we come in contact with. With His presence we can reflect the SON.

WE ARE IN GOOD HANDS

I remember my two sisters and I going outside to play. Our mom wanted us to play where we could be seen by her out the window. She always kept a close watch on us to make sure we were safe. Our Heavenly Father keeps a close watch on us also. I love the words to the old hymn that says "His eye is on the sparrow and I know He watches me". In Psalms 34:15 it reads "the eyes of the Lord are upon the righteous…" He never takes His eyes off of you and me. Wherever we go; whatever we do He is watching. I'm thankful for a great God who cares so much about you and me. We are in good hands with God.

←—————————————→

DELAY IS NOT DENIAL

Our family would go to Kentucky to visit my aunt and uncle for a few days. Many times on the way we would get stopped by a train at a railroad crossing that held us up for a long time. I was anxious to get to their home and put this train behind us. In life there are things that put our life on hold. At times our life can seem like it's at a stand-still. A lot of times God allows things to happen for a reason. But we will not be on hold forever. Our life will proceed when God has done what He felt was best for us. Delay does not mean denial; it sometimes means there's something better ahead.

←—————————————→

WALKING BY FAITH

My husband and I have always loved going to the Smoky Mountains. One day we had been up in the mountains and were heading back down. It was dark and getting late. There was a heavy fog that caused visibility to be difficult. Mike had to stop and figure out where we were. Isn't that a lot like us sometimes? There are days that everything seems clear to us; but other days when everything seems foggy. It's then we have to walk by faith. When we are walking in faith; we are trusting in God completely. Even if we don't see what lies ahead; we can know God is going before us and making the way clear.

SPICE UP YOUR LIFE 136

I have made zucchini bread lots of times. Mike does not like zucchini; but loves the bread. Isn't it amazing how you can take a vegetable you don't like and make something so delicious? A lot of things in life are not so appealing when you are going thru it; but God can take a difficult time in our life and turn it around for a beautiful time in our life. Many people who have lived a sinful life, come to God and their life becomes more beautiful. God has a way of adding "spice" to a life-completely changing it. Only God can "spice" up a life and make it more appealing.

WE SAW THE LIGHT 137

Several years ago we took our group of widows to the Smoky Mountains the early part of December. We went and rode "Ober Gatlinburg". As we rode up we could see the snow coming down. The ladies really enjoyed it; but none of us wanted to be stuck up there. When we came down there was snow everywhere. As we were leaving the area back to Pigeon Forge-all the lights went out in the city. We looked back and all we could see was darkness. As Christians we can look back and see where sin brought darkness into our life. But when we met Jesus-He changed our life completely and we saw the light. What a glorious experience.

WHAT A DIFFERENCE 138

I remember a song I used to hear called "What A Difference You've Made In My Life". The song was made popular in the 70's by Ronnie Milsap; but later it was made into a gospel song by Amy Grant. There are many people in life that have made a difference in my life. My husband; parents; sisters; preachers; and many friends. All these are "tops" in my books for helping me get to where I am now. But there's only one that impacted my life the most. The Lord has made the biggest difference and completely changed my life. Yes what a difference He's made in my life. And He can do the same for you.

FRUITS IN OUR DIET 139

There are some fruits I like; but I'm not a big fruit eater. However, I do know that fruit is good for us. I like bananas, peaches, grapes and strawberries. The Bible speaks of the fruit of the spirit that will impact our life. Matthew 7:17 says "every good tree bears good fruit". Picking fruit from a tree, you must be very careful that they are not rotten or eaten with insects. Our life must bear the fruit mentioned in Galatians 5:22-23 "Love, joy, peace, longsuffering, faith, gentleness, goodness, meekness, temperance". We could all use help in making these a part of our life everyday. Every Christian should display these fruits in their life daily.

A GIFT FOR YOU

Most people enjoy getting a gift. I've watched people open a gift not wanting to tear the paper. I always want to say "here, let me help you" as they tear it carefully so they can preserve the wrapping. Its not the size of the package, but what's inside it; as well as how it was picked just for me. My husband and I have learned how rewarding it is to give, rather than to receive. The Bible says "It's more blessed to give than to receive". I heard a minister say one time when you "cast your bread upon the water" you can expect it back soggy or buttered. In fact it will come back as a gift to you-very tasty.

WELL DONE

When going to ministerial training, I learned a lot from some great Godly teachers and ministers. Every time we went to a class, my husband and I would have to take a test. I, for one, am not crazy about taking a test. At the end of all the seminars, I had to take a final test of 300 questions. Believe me, I didn't look forward to it at all. Everyone of us have gone thru some "test" in our life. They are not pleasant either; but one thing I have learned, to have a testimony, you must go thru a test. So just look past any test you are going thru to see the testimony that awaits to be shared with others along the way.

THE GREAT HOMECOMING

Many people go to family reunions. It's there we see family members we haven't seen in a long time. It's so good to see each of them; and see how the children have grown. Churches used to have homecomings with dinner on the grounds and a gospel singing in the afternoon. I look forward to the day when we all get together in Heaven. We will all be happy as we see those who have gone on before us. I love the song "I Want To Stroll Over Heaven With You". I can only imagine what it will be like as we walk the streets of gold with our loved ones. One that I look forward to is seeing Jesus. What a great Homecoming Day that will be.

CARRIED BY THE FATHER 143

We've been to Florida many times to visit good friends there. I love walking along the beach and watching the tide come in. Many times as I walked across the sand, I would look back and see my footprints vanishing with the water. That's a lot like you and me when we are going thru a tough time in our life. We can see the water coming in and we feel we are overwhelmed and about to drown. I'm thankful the Lord is right there with us all the way. It's then our Heavenly Father picks us up and carries us. It's then we have nothing to fear. My friend we can make it when we are carried by HIM.

NOT PERFECT-JUST FORGIVEN 144

Paul in the Bible is an example of someone who was not perfect. But one day his life changed and turned around. His past was not good at all; but he learned to "forget the past and press on". A lot of Christians have a hard time of letting go of their past. When we let go we will experience a freedom in our walk with God. Paul said it well when he said "that I may know Him". Do we really know Him…down deep in our heart? When we really get to know Him, we will understand that God doesn't look for perfection-just forgiveness. It's a proven fact that none of us are perfect; but it is for sure we are forgiven

THE LITTLE FOXES 145

When I was a little girl I got a thorn in the bottom of my foot. Even though I didn't want it removed, it made a difference in my walking when my dad got it out. The little things can hinder our walk with the Lord. We try to ignore it…but it doesn't go away. We must realize we must give it all to God so He can remove it. The "little things" can make a big difference if they aren't taken care of. There's a scripture that says it's the "little foxes that spoil the vines". Song of Solomon 2:15. It's time you and I let go of those things that hinder our "walk" with Him. In God's eyes there are no little or big things. They are all the same size to Him.

HE IS THE ANSWER 146

We've all tried to call someone on the phone but couldn't get in touch with them. Either we got a busy signal, a recording or no answer at all. I'm so thankful it isn't like that with God. I'm thankful "His ears are open to our cry" anytime of the day. Some people are said to have "selective hearing". Aren't we glad our Heavenly Father is completely different from that? A man once wrote "God is the answer". Someone else wrote under it "what's the question"? Another person wrote under that "it doesn't matter". How true that is. He is the answer to everything!

LIVING ON THE EDGE 147

Mike and I have been to Fall Creek Falls state park a few times. There's a certain point you can stand on the edge to overlook the beauty there. I remember standing there and my husband told me to back up and not stand so close to the edge. A lot of times in life if we aren't careful, we will live on the edge; but we must always be under His protection and away from the things of this world. It may have a beautiful view, but it could cause us to "fall" for something that will draw us away from God and His blessings. Never live on the edge; but in the shelter of His arms.

←—————————————————→

WHERE WE ARE-HE'S THERE 148

We've all heard the saying "you can take the girl out of the country; but you can't take the country out of the girl". I was raised in the country when I was young. One day working as a phone operator at the Medical Office, I answered the phone and a gentleman on the other end of the line said "I like your accent. What is it?" It caught me off guard. I wasn't aware I had an accent, so I just answered "country". My husband and I live in the city now. One thing I've learned is it doesn't matter where we are; who we are is still inside us. The same it is in our life. If we are a child of God, we should be the same person doesn't matter where it is. If Christ lives in us, we are a new creature in Him.

←—————————————————→

HOW COOL IS THAT 149

My sister and I work in the yard often. While out there I may not notice all the dirt on me until I come inside; but it's then I know I need to get cleaned up. It feels so good to get into the shower and all the sweat and dirt be washed away. That soap, body wash and the water makes a big difference getting rid of the dirt and trash. When we became a Christian we were cleansed from a lot of trash. Jesus' blood did a lot better job than soap and water. "What can wash away my sins? Nothing but the blood of Jesus". Just as a shower or a hot bath makes us feel so clean…so much better is the cleansing from our Lord. How cool is that!

$$\longleftrightarrow$$

NOT JUST HISTORY-BUT OUR FUTURE 150

Years ago we flew to California to visit my niece and her family. It was our first visit there. They decided to take us to Virginia City, Nevada-an old western town with a lot of history; built on the side of a mountain. You could sense the steps of people in the past on those old wooden sidewalks. I've heard stories of preachers of the past; and Christians who wrote hymns. Each had a story to tell. The stories of Jesus over 2000 years ago never grows old. It's new every time I read it or hear it read. Those stories will never be outdated because they are not just history but our future.

$$\longleftrightarrow$$

HE'S IN CONTROL 151

My sister and I took one of my nieces to Kentucky for her birthday many years ago. There was no crowd so we decided to ride the "Cup". It started out slow; but gained speed the more we went. My sister and niece kept sliding. It was so funny. We kept yelling "stop this thing"; but could not get the operator's attention. That's a lot like our life. Everything seems "smooth" then from nowhere, things seem out of control spinning around. We know it's there but we can't find the "control button". We cry out to Jesus and all is calm. We may have forgotten, but He was in control all the time.

MAKE OUT YOUR LIST 152

Growing up in the country, we didn't go to town when we ran out of something. We had to buy ahead of time. But on Tuesday a peddler came thru the rural routes with items we may need. My mom would look to see what things we needed. I always loved it when he came. I was very small; so dad would pick me up and sit me on the truck to pick out something. In life we don't have to be without anything. We can make out our list and tell God. He knows what we need before we even pray; but He still wants us to ask in faith for it. Isn't it amazing that Jesus is passing your way…not just on Tuesday but everyday?

SING YOUR SONG 153

My husband and I used to go camping a lot. It was so enjoyable to be out in the nature world. While camping we met some wonderful people. On one occasion we met a couple of teachers who invited us to their campsite one night. One of them played the guitar while they sang a song they had written about us. That was so special to my husband and me. It was a great night as we sat around the fire. God reminds me He can give us a song regardless of where we are or what's going on in our life… in the day or in the night. It's time we sing the song God has given to us. The fire inside of us will burn on and on.

DON'T LOSE IT 154

In the Mountains, my husband and I went to a picnic area to have a picnic. We saw some guys standing back from their table and wondered what was going on. As we approached we saw a bear in the middle of their table. These guys had cooked big steaks on the grill and the bear was enjoying every bite. Every time we are enjoying the blessings of God, the enemy tries to step in-distract us-and steal our blessings. The sad thing about it is we will let him because of fear. Remember Satan comes to steal, kill and destroy; but God comes to give us life more abundantly. Don't be afraid. Enjoy every "bite" of the blessings of the Lord.

$$\longleftrightarrow$$

WHAT ARE YOU SEARCHING FOR? 155

Our family was staying in a cabin in the Mountains some years ago. One night we heard a lot of noise out on the porch. We decided to look out and see what was happening. We were shocked to see there were raccoons trying to get into the trash cans. They were making every effort possible to get the cans open. People are searching for something to satisfy their life. Like the raccoons they are still trying to find a way to "open" the door. Many try on their own to make it happen or they look in all the wrong places. I can tell you now what we are searching for won't be found in a garbage can.

$$\longleftrightarrow$$

THE FLOW OF THE HOLY SPIRIT 156

I've always enjoyed going to Fall Creek Falls State Park. They have a waterfall there that is about 256ft tall. I recall going there one time when the waterfall wasn't very pretty. It was because they hadn't had much rain. The more rain the more water comes down that waterfall. That reminds me of our walk with God when we haven't experienced the "rain" of the Holy Spirit in our life. You can experience this when you sit in His presence and spend time with Him. The Holy Spirit is like a "cleaning agent" as well as a "cool drink" on a dry land. That woman at Jacob's well experienced that; and you and I can too.

JUNK OR TREASURE 157

I really like going to yard sales. I've found some really neat things at great prices. "Someone's junk becomes someone else's treasure" is so true. One spring we took our widow's group to Watertown to a city-wide yard sale. It's amazing the things we came back with. Most Christians can say when they got saved they traded a lot of "junk" for "treasures" in Heaven. It was junk we didn't want; and nothing anyone else would want. Like yardsale items they were tired of it all. It was a lot of baggage they were hanging on to. But Jesus took it without any argument and paid the ultimate price.

THE PRESSURE 158

My husband bought me a pressure cooker several years ago; but I never used it. The old ones were known for accidents from the pressure; and the steam could be dangerous. A lot of people are like the old pressure cookers. When under pressure they blow up or let off a lot of steam. But like food cooked in the pressure cooker; the pressures of life can cause us to become soft and tender before God if we let it. My mom always said "a soft answer turneth away wrath". The next time you feel pressure in your life, see which cooker best describes you. Would it be the old one or the new?

CAST YOUR VOTE 159

Election day is a very important day in our country. Many become upset and disappointed if the ending count is not what we wanted. Regardless of how the results come out; one thing for sure God is still in control. I was reminded how He is the Overseer; the Supervisor; the Administrator and CEO of our Universe. Nothing will change that and no one can take His place. He has my vote. 2 Peter 1:10 reads "give diligence to make your calling and election sure; for if you do these things, you shall never fall." Just think: God reigns today and forevermore.

HEED THE WARNING 160

We went to several zoos with our young nieces years ago. There's some big animals there. I remember the tall giraffes and large elephants. I thought about how big the Ark must have been when Noah built it. I admire Noah building the Ark even when the people said "it's not going to rain". But Noah took God's Word and obeyed Him. Many sermons have been preached about Jesus coming back. You can tell most people don't believe it by they way they are living. But look around friend. Things are pointing to His return. The rain came in Noah's day; and I can tell you Jesus is coming too. His return will be when most people are not looking for Him.

WHERE IS IT?

Have you ever put something in a "safe place" and went back to get it and it wasn't there? We will look and look and then back-track our steps trying to find it. When I can't find something, I've learned to stop, sit down, pray and ask God where it is. It's amazing I will go back to where I've looked before and there it will be. In the hustle of our life we must ask "where did I lose the joy of living? Where could it be"? It's then we must stop, sit down, take a deep breath and pray. You'll find everything that's missing in His presence. In fact it will be right where you left it.

ONLY YOU

My husband and I have gone to two Marriage Encounter weekends during our marriage. We sat under Lead Couples and listened as they shared what they had been thru as a couple. These weren't for bad marriages; but to make good marriages better. At these weekends we could not use phones or watch TV. This was a time you focused only on your mate and God. How rewarding it would be if we would take time off from our phones, facebook, TV's and computers; to have an "encounter" with God...just the two of us. What a difference it would make in our relationship with Him.

SURPRISED

Have you ever been surprised by receiving a gift you were not expecting? Maybe something you needed or would just "like to have". Maybe it was something you had wanted for a long time. Out of nowhere they come your way. These are what I call "unexpected blessings from God." Our God has ways of bringing little "nuggets of gold" along our way to show His love to us. He can use people like you and me to bring kindness to others. Never forget to be thankful for friends God sends your way…for they are "treasures" from up above.

FOLLOW YOUR INSTINCTS 164

It's heart-warming to see how God has given animals the instinct of what to do when cold and bad weather approaches. Bears go into hibernation; squirrels start hiding walnuts for the winter days ahead; and geese will fly south to find warmer weather. God provides food for the little birds in the winter time, even if there seems to be no food in sight. If God cares for the little sparrow that falls to the ground; how much more does our heavenly Father care for you and me. Follow the instinct God has given you. He will give guidance in every season of our life and He will take care of us!

EXCUSES 165

The Kingsmen Quartet sang a song called "Excuses" years ago. The song said "excuses, excuses, you hear them everyday". Have you ever heard someone make an excuse for their child; telling why they didn't do something they were supposed to do? I wonder how God views excuses made. Does He view it as dishonesty? When it comes to the things of God He wants us to do, He makes a way for us to do it…no excuses please. How do people perceive our honesty and integrity? Charles Stanley said it well: "If we are busy and full of excuses, remember someone's eternal destiny is at stake." There's really no excuse for excuses, is there?

SENIORS ARE SPECIAL

The older I get the more I love the older generation-probably because I have now joined their group. Mike and I have talked how we always enjoy spending time with them; and have received great advice from many of them. There is much wisdom to be gleaned from them. Ruth loved Naomi, her mother-in-law and wanted to cling to her; that wherever she went she wanted to be there. My husband and I love working with Seniors and being a part of their lives. They bless us! Today reach out to any senior God places on your heart. They are waiting for your call and you will make their day.

←——————————————→

CHECK UP OR TUNE UP

Our vehicles need repair work done to make it run better. They may need an oil-change to get rid of the bad oil or even a new oil filter. This helps our vehicles operate much better. My husband taught me to watch for warning lights. In our walk with the Lord-we get warning signs meaning we need a check-up. The "little things" hinders us in this race. It could be a "tune-up" with our attitude; thought-life; or priorities with God. We can go to God without an appointment and get this taken care of immediately. The best part is it's free.

←——————————————→

BE KIND

I saw on the News several days ago a story about two young girls who made a difference in their small town. They were painting signs with the words BE KIND on them. People started buying their signs all over town. Their signs now can be seen in yards all over their city. The mayor posted a big sign at the entrance of their city reading "Kindness- Capitol of Kentucky". Also a BE KIND sign was posted at Times Square in Manhattan. Good deeds and acts of kindness can lift one's spirit and go a long way. Ephesians 4:32 reads "Be kind one to another." Let's show some kindness today. Our spirit will be lifted because of it.

JUST LIKE HIM 169

Have you ever thought you would like to be just like someone else? I see people with strong faith, a strong prayer life, and even people with great wisdom, and I think I want to be just like them. I realize there's only one way I can really do that, and this song says it best: "To be like Jesus, to be like Jesus. All I ask is to be like Him. All thru life's journey, from earth to Heaven. All I ask is to be like Him." All that really matters is to make sure we walk in His steps and be more like Him every day. Lets make this our prayer and desire today. We can't go wrong being like Him.

ALL ABOARD 170

One year my husband and I went on the Broadway Dinner Train for our anniversary. We boarded the train in Nashville and settled in for a new adventure. As we began to travel, the meal of soup, salad, entrée and dessert were served. That 2.5 hour dinner-train ride will always be in our book of memories. As we look back over our life we count our blessings. We've "climbed aboard" experiences we haven't seen before; but God went with us for the ride. He has served some "entrees" of hope and some "sweet memories" along the way. We can look back and say "Wow! What a ride that was!"

LEAVING A LEGACY

Several years ago my mom went to be with the Lord. Many times I sat at her table and received great advice from her. She was full of faith and wisdom. Mom was a friend to all; and never spoke evil of anyone. She prayed fervently for her family; for all her friends and for any need that arose. She believed with all her heart in the power of prayer; and she got answers in return. What a legacy she left for her children; grandchildren; and great grandchildren. Think about it. What will people remember us for? The greatest legacy is our faith in God. It's more valuable than money.

$$\longleftrightarrow$$

A PENCIL OF FAITH

When I was in first grade they gave my parents a list of supplies to buy. I was given a very fat pencil to use. They believed first graders could grip and hold it tighter and be less likely to drop it and make it easier to learn to write. This is relative to our walk with Christ. If our faith is "big" we can have a tighter grip on God and we won't drop all our values, dreams and goals that mean a lot in our walk with God. Our story can be written easier as we hold tightly to the Big God we serve. Pick up your "pencil of faith" and continue your life-story. One day, someone will pick it up and read it.

$$\longleftrightarrow$$

CHOICES

We have all chosen what to do in our life including a career to embark upon. We've made choices regarding buying a car, truck or home. Choices we make affect not only our life but others in our life. The greatest choice we could make was making the Lord our Savior. If you are at a crossroads in your life where a decision needs to be made; I recommend you make the choice to seek God for the answer. He can give us the direction we need and show us the way. Every choice we make is critical in our day-to-day living. So choose prayerfully.

DON'T HOLD TOO TIGHTLY 174

I've shared how I would go with dad to get some small pigs and would hold one tightly in the back seat all the way home. When they were big-my dad with some friends-would kill them so we could have fresh and smoked meat for the winter. I knew better than to get "attached" to them; because I knew they would be on our table for a meal. We must not get too "attached" to "things" in life. These may start out "little" but can become "big" fast. "Things" can draw us away from God instead of to God. I recommend we hold to "things" loosely. It's ok to have things, if things don't have us.

NO MORE HUNTING 175

Growing up I was a daddy's girl and loved to go hunting with him. When I was old enough, my dad bought me a small rifle and taught we how to squirrel and rabbit hunt. I really enjoyed the fried rabbit "I killed" and the gravy and homemade biscuits my mom had prepared. Most of us have hunted for things to satisfy the "hunger" missing in our life. Many people look for what they need in the wrong places. We can try a lot of things; but "only Jesus can satisfy our soul". If you are on a hunt… search no more. I know because once I found Jesus my hunting days were over.

SHOWING LOVE

I taught the second grade Sunday School class for years. The students were always engrossed with the stories of the Bible. One young boy was noisy and loud; always distracting the class. One Sunday my husband picked him up over his shoulder; took him in the hall to speak to him. Sitting the boy down, the young boy surprised my husband by saying "do that again". My husband replied "doesn't your dad do that?" His answer was no. We used him in our class as my helper. He became one of the best kids in the class. People are hurting, just needing our love. What the world needs is love....our love and God's love.

PAST BLESSINGS

Growing up, holidays were very special to me.
You could smell the sweet potato pie and the chicken and dressing being prepared to eat. As we sat around the table we were thankful for what God had given us. Jesus was the head of our home. As we reflect over the past; may each of us be mindful of the many blessings God has given to us. We all have so much to thank God for. As my mom always said "Look back and count your blessings". We should all make sure we have a thankful heart and give thanks with a grateful heart.

FRIENDS ARE A BLESSING

One event stands out in my mind. My older sister and her family were living out of state and my dad had passed away a few years before. I remember a special friend inviting us to go with her to the "Mess Hall" at Ft Campbell . Her husband was stationed out of state. We had never been there before. That was an exciting day and what a meal we had! There was so much food to choose from. I am so thankful for family and friends. Money won't buy true friendship. It's something God has given to us to enjoy. Treasure all your friends today.

A HEART OF THANKFULNESS 179

I remember Nov. 6, 2006 when my husband had a heart attack and was dead for 4 ½ minutes. Two days later he had open-heart surgery. After he came home, we were getting ready to go to my mom and sister's home for Thanksgiving lunch. As my husband was taking a shower I heard him yell for me. I hurried to the bathroom and found him "out of it". God helped me get him out of the shower to sit down. He was suppose to sit down to shower but was not told. My mom and sister brought the meal to our home that Thanksgiving. Do I have things to be thankful for? You better believe it!

WE ARE BLESSED 180

A man told a pastor "I'm finished with this Christian walk and living for God. I am quitting". The pastor said "before you quit write down all that God has done for you this past year". Two weeks later the man came to his pastor "I changed my mind, I'm not going to quit because I'm still writing my blessings down.". I agree. I must brag on my best friend: JESUS. He's my silver lining around the clouds; the Lily in my valley; my rainbow after every storm; the Rose of Sharon; my bright and morning star. We are blessed more than we deserve. We should be thankful every day.

STANDING IN LINE 181

"Black Friday" is known as the busiest shopping day. My husband and I used to stand in line early in the morning to be one of the first 100 shoppers to get a free gift card. I remember one year very early in the morning as we stood outside the store it was so cold that my niece brought us two chairs and throws. I heard the guy in front of us say "I wish I had a niece like that". In God's book there are no "black Fridays" and we don't have to stand in line for over an hour to receive from God. He said He would give us "the desires of our heart" and that's something department stores can't always fulfill.

SOON IT WILL BE HERE 182

To a child it seems Birthdays will never come; but to us older folk it's here before we know it. In fact it sneaks up on us. The Bible speaks of us becoming as a child. We must have a child-like faith and their zeal. As a child looks forward to birthdays, we should have that same anticipation for His return. Children look for a gift or gifts for their birthday; but we look for our "perfect gift" coming in the sky. Yes Jesus is coming. Many people don't believe it. They say they have heard it all their life. That means it is just that much closer. If you ask me, His return would be the best gift ever.

IT'S MORE BLESSED TO GIVE 183

There's a commercial Mike and I love. A dad and his son are eating in a diner. Their waitress tells another waitress about some financial issues she's having. The dad puts a piece of money down on his bill as they leave. Outside the son says "dad you left a hundred dollar bill". The dad replied "it's ok son-I'll get it back". The son said "I don't understand" and the father replies "one day you will". Luke 6:38 says "give and it shall be given unto you". It's not how much we give; but how it's given from our heart. Now that's the true spirit of giving.

A LITTLE MORE TIME 184

My husband's uncle came to live here in our town for a while from Colorado. He went to church with us and we went out to eat often. Sometimes we would encounter people that would "try our patience". His comment was "we just got to give them a little more time". I've thought of his words very often. I'm thankful God didn't give up on us or "write us off". I can hear Him say "I will give them a little more time; they will come around ". He is so longsuffering and patient. The next time someone gets on your nerves just "give them a little more time". You will have a satisfaction feeling in your heart.

PAY FORWARD 185

I heard someone sharing about going thru a drive-up to get a sandwich and soda. When they got up there to pay, the lady informed him the person in front had already paid for the food; so he decided to pay for the person behind him. That's what they call "pay forward". I was thinking about that and couldn't help but think how God did the same for us. We owed a debt we couldn't pay; but God "paid forward" that debt He didn't owe. It occurred on a rugged cross on Calvary's hill. That's what we call "Amazing Grace". That debt was paid over 2000 years ago. So amazing!

THE CHRISTMAS TREE 186

One year I put up a tree decorated with angels all over it. It was a simple tree; but I really liked the different angels on the top and all over the tree. I worked in a dept store when I was in high school. There was a talking Christmas tree as you walked in the door that the children loved. My supervisor and I decorated trees with different themes. People would buy them "as is" and we would decorate another one. One tree changed my life with no ornaments, garland or tinsel; with one light on it "the light of the world-Jesus". No tree in our home will ever impact us like that tree. May we always include Him in our home.

$$\longleftrightarrow$$

THE GREATEST PARADE 187

I remember the first Christmas parade in our city. It was a cold night and people everywhere. My dad picked me up so I could see the floats; bands, clowns and other sites. This event will always be in my memory growing up as a young girl. Imagine the parade we will have in Heaven. Saints lining the streets of Gold. The heavenly host praising their savior. The Master of ceremonies will be Jesus. Our attention will be on Him. And guess what? We will be escorted by Him. If you love parades don't miss this one. It will be "out of this world" and will last forever!

$$\longleftrightarrow$$

LET IT SNOW-LET IT SNOW 188

I love living where there is four seasons. A fresh fallen snow in the winter looks so pure. You can look across the yard and see no dirt; sticks; leaves or footprints; just pure white snow. The snow reminds me of God's forgiveness and love. My husband loves the scripture in Isaiah 1:18 that says "though your sins be as scarlet, they shall be white as snow". When God forgives, there is no blemishes or stains left. "What can wash away my sin? Nothing but the blood of Jesus. ..Oh precious is the flow that makes me white as snow." My prayer is "Create in me a clean heart O God". Psalms 51

LITTLE SURPRISES 189

I made some coconut bon-bon candy that were so pretty and really did taste good. They were very easy to make. They have a "surprise" ingredient in them you wouldn't expect…cold mashed potatoes. I thought of how Jesus surprises each of us often like a call that "just makes our day" and "lifts our spirit". Or we may receive mail that "surprises" us and is "the icing on the cake". God sends "little nuggets of gold" or "little jewels" to "pick us up" or "warm our heart". Don't take for granted the "little things" He sends your way. He loves to "surprise" His children.

LIGHT YOUR CANDLE 190

Most of us use candles in our home. They come in handy when there is a power-outage. People have used candles to read by at night-time. Beginning in the 1800's people put candles on their Christmas tree; but they were hard to keep attached to the tree. They were kept lit only 30minutes at a time to prevent a fire. Buckets of sand or water were kept nearby in case of fire. We represent candles in a dark world. We are the only "light" many people see. Don't let "things" of this world put out that light. Let's be the "candle" to represent Jesus to others. "This little light of mine, I'm gonna let it shine".

BEYOND THE WREATH   191

I used to decorate wreaths. My husband pulled the vines down and made the wreaths for me. I would use ribbons and other items to make the wreath appealing to sell. The wreath can represent a "circle of unending love". Before I decorated those wreaths, it reminded me of the crown my Savior wore at Calvary. It wasn't beautiful or decorated but represented pain. It was a symbol of God's love…God's unending love for all of us. As you hang a wreath on your door; over your mantle; or anywhere in your house; let it remind you how much God loves you by sending His Son to wear that crown. Amazing Love!

SING IT OUT!   192

Year before last all my family came to our house a few days before Christmas for a meal. After we ate my nieces and nephews started singing Christmas carols. On the spur of the moment, we decided to go caroling to our neighbors. It was so heartwarming as we heard the comments and saw the smiles. One couple said "why don't people do this more often"? I will say it sure can lift the spirits of others. There are "tokens of love" we can share with others that don't cost anything. The Heavenly host sang aloud of Jesus birth. As we share love with others; we too will have a song in our heart that can bring Joy To The World!

PRECIOUS GIFTS

I was thinking about gift-giving and how fun it can be. Growing up the gifts given to us girls were bought with love and were special to us. My husband and I decided several years ago to not buy gifts for each other; but to invest in someone else's Christmas. We prayed God would show us what family to buy gifts for. We were so excited as we shopped for this family. It's the best feeling you can ever experience. God taught us it is all about giving and sharing; for God gave His best….His Son.

HE NEVER CHANGES

Our family comes to our house for a meal and lots of fun for Christmas. It's always so good to see the family together laughing and joking around. I started a tradition of playing games and putting on skits after we eat. Then we exchange gifts. There have been some changes over the years; even the meals we cook. Some changes are good; but some are not that easy. But I'm glad Jesus never changes. It's all about Him anyway. It is still our Savior's birthday; and He will always be in our heart and midst.

CELEBRATE EVERYDAY

I love to celebrate the birth of Christ. It seems people love each other more; they are more courteous and sensitive to the feelings of others; and more joyful and happy in their spirit. These should not only be expressed once a year. I think we should experience these feelings everyday. We should be mindful of the feelings of others and sensitive to their needs.

I believe God wants us to spread more joy along the way. Our world would be a better place. Instead of hate, show love. Instead of fear, spread peace; and center everything around Jesus.

I BELIEVE IN MIRACLES 196

I am a firm believer in miracles. My husband and I have experienced miracles in our lives and I know the power behind every miracle. Miracles don't just happen on a certain day. We experience a miracle every time we rise up in the morning; take a breath; view a sunrise or sunset; or see a newborn baby. I know miracles are real and they happen to all those who believe. But the greatest miracle is when a person is saved. A hymn says it best: "But when He saved my soul; cleansed and made me whole. It took a miracle of love and grace." Believe today for your miracle.

NEW STAR SHINING 197

I've told many times about living in the country as a young girl and seeing all the stars in the sky. Psalms 147:4 says "He tells the number of stars; He calleth them by their name". There was a star in the sky that led the shepherds to where Jesus was born. I sometimes wonder what the name of that star was. Matt 2:2 reads " we have seen His star in the east and come to worship him". That star can lead us all to our Savior as well. I love that song because it says "if we want to find it-I know we will. For that new star is shining for us still". Friend if you look hard enough, you will see it shining in your life.

DON'T BE AFRAID TO SAY IT

198

Growing up I remember bell ringers outside of the businesses downtown. I also remember going into the "five and dime" stores and hearing people proclaim "Merry Christmas" . You could feel the excitement in the air. I never understood how we got away from those two words. Without Christ there would be no Christmas. Saying "Merry Christmas" is like saying "Jesus is the reason for the season". Those words are more than a tradition; they are reality. We can make a difference by saying "Merry Christmas". Let's be determined to be the people to declare this to others.

← —————————— →

GOD WITH US

199

I can read the Christmas story and Easter story anytime of the year. Matthew 1:23 says "behold a virgin shall be with child and shall bring forth a son and they shall call his name Emmanuel, which being interpreted is 'God with us'". He is our Emmanuel. He is with us in the good times and the bad; in sickness and in health. He was with us in our yesterdays; He'll be with us in our tomorrows; and He is with us today. We are never alone. He will be with us every step of the way because He really is our Emmanuel-God with us! I am so thankful He is alive and with us forever.

← —————————— →

IT'S NOT FANTASY

200

I usually make candies and sweets to share with family and friends. I made some fantasy fudge yesterday. This candy is so delicious and easy to make. When I was making this candy,

I was reminded how many people live in a fantasy world; a lifestyle of "illusion" and "imagination". I'm thankful, as Christians, we don't have to imagine what our life or outcome will be. We can know for sure. We serve a God of reality and we know God has promised good things to those who love Him. He has a plan for each of our lives. To me that is much better than fantasy fudge.

PLUGGED IN AND FILLED UP 201

Years ago I had "bubble lights" I would put them on our tree when Christmas came around. I would plug them in and watch as they bubbled up in those little tubes. My nieces were always fascinated with them. I was reminded of a scripture that says "from your belly shall flow rivers of living water" John 7:38. A chorus we sing says "spring up O well within my soul". As we allow the Holy Spirit to fill our being; it will "bubble up" and overflow. Just as the bubble-lights, our life will attract others. But we must be "plugged in" to the source: Jesus.

THE LIGHT NOT SEASONAL 202

I love the beautiful lights on the trees downtown; especially during the Christmas season. Our little dog is even fascinated with them. She will sit up real tall in my lap observing them. I was thinking of how beautiful Heaven will be when we get there. It will be "lit" up but not from street lights. Rev 21:23 says "the city had no need of the sun…the moon to shine in it…the glory of God did lighten it and the lamb is the light thereof". Rev 22:5 says "no need of a candle…for the Lord God giveth them light". It's beyond our imagination and it definitely won't be seasonal either! I look forward to "sitting up" and observing all the beauty.

THRU THE EYES OF A CHILD 203

People of all ages like to build Ginger-bread houses or decorate cookies. I have done that as well. In fact it makes a person feel like a child again. The Bible speaks of us becoming as a little child. Matt 18:3 says "except you become as little children, ye shall not enter the kingdom of Heaven." A child's faith is simple and honest; and their love is genuine. Their heart is pure and forgives and will love the unlovable. They have simple faith that we all need to have. I believe we should see every day God gives us as through the eyes of a child.

NOT AS IT APPEARS 204

One of my favorite dishes I prepare is called Kraut Slaw. You may say "I don't like kraut". Honestly, you will never taste the kraut. The red pimentos and green peppers add color to this dish. I've noticed people often-times will voice their opinion on things without really trying it or discovering it. Many people have that same outlook on salvation and the things of God. People that have not had this experience, don't really know what they are missing. It's the best life that one can live. If you want to serve a beautiful dish for your guest-make the kraut slaw; but if you want to share a beautiful life-serve God.

TAKE JESUS WITH YOU

Many people don't feel successful in their walk with God. They will say they can't sing, teach or witness like they should. I'm reminded of Mary the mother of Jesus, an handmaiden of the Lord who was visited by an angel; who informed her she would be carrying the Savior. Her reply was "how can this be"? She was told that "with God nothing shall be impossible". She was a young girl chosen by God to do this mission. God can use you "just as you are". As we carry Jesus in our heart others will see the "real" Jesus. Let's allow Him to change us just as Mary was completely changed by Christ.

$$\longleftrightarrow$$

CARRY ON

When Christmas comes around I usually make Christmas Wreaths made like Rice Krispie treats, except I use cornflakes and a few drops of green food coloring. I shape them into wreaths and put 3-4 redhots on the wreath. Some of my nieces have carried over this tradition and make them for their family. My parents left a legacy I want to carry on and leave behind. I feel their genuine love and strong faith must be carried on from one generation to another. We all must leave strong values that can be carried on by those who are following in our footsteps.

$$\longleftrightarrow$$

INVEST IN A CHILD

My husband and I have been involved with two children's homes within the 40 years of our marriage. We've seen the hurt and disappointment in the eyes of many children; but we've also seen the joy and smiles come back into their lives when they get to know the Lord. I am a firm believer when you invest in a child, you invest in eternity. When you take time for your children and your grandchildren, you will never be disappointed. Your investment in their lives, can bring them to the Lord and change their life completely.

THE STORY GOES ON 208

I never get tired of the stories of Christ. I've heard sermons about Christ and testimonies and songs about Him. Jesus has made such a big difference in my life. He's not in the manger but He lives in my heart. He's not in the grave, but alive. It's not a myth but reality. He's not the past but He is in my present. Many lives have been changed by Him. He wasn't born in an elite motel; but He wants His best for us. We must carry this story on. There are millions who are looking for hope and for an answer; and how will they know if we don't share this story to everyone we meet. Yes, this story must go on.

THE PERFECT GIFT 209

We've all been at a place when we looked for the perfect gift for someone; something unique and special. We search and never are satisfied with what we find. To be honest it's hard to buy a gift for someone who has everything. There is only one perfect gift that is suitable for any occasion. A song says it well: "I give you Jesus. He's the one that surpasses all understanding. I give you Jesus. He's the water that you drink and never thirst again". The best gift anyone can receive from us is Jesus. He's not just for special occasions; but every day of the year. A gift that keeps on giving!

SECURE AND SAFE

We really can't take life for granted. It is full of changes and so much uncertainty. It is imperative we hold to God's unchanging hand. Earthly things will fade away; but His name will last forever. He is strong and powerful in adversity. We can call on His name in the time of trouble. Proverbs 18:10 says "the name of the Lord is a strong tower; the righteous runneth into it and is safe". As a mother hen gathers her chicks under her wings for safety; so are we sheltered in the arms of God. He is our refuge. He is our help and all we will ever need. So don't you fear, child of God. He is with us.

SWEETER AND SWEETER

After a vacation; holiday or special event, some people have a "let-down" feeling. Sometimes the weather and temperatures keep many inside their homes. After the festivities or events we plan are over; it's good to know the excitement of Christ never ends. In fact, every day with Him, gets brighter and more enjoyable. I urge each of us to keep Christ close in our day-to-day activities. We need Him every second; every moment; and every day of our life. He is an on-time God. Let's not take one step without Him; but keep Him active in our daily life; because He "gets sweeter and sweeter as the days go by".

MEETING THE CHALLENGE

As we look over the year, we can see many challenges we have encountered. Some may not have been so pleasant for us or others we love. It's not easy to see our friends and loved ones going thru some difficult times. To be honest life isn't always easy. Sickness, death and hardships can bring sadness; but I'm glad we know someone who will bring us thru every challenge we face; and He is the joy of our salvation. Many challenges come our way, but with God's help we can meet it head-on. Thru every test, be assured we can find a testimony awaiting us.

RUN TO JESUS 213

We've heard the saying "if life gives you lemons-make lemon-aide". In difficult situations we can either run to God or away from Him. My husband and I have experienced many trials along the way; but we've always turned to God. It's during those times we can experience a close relationship with Him. God uses difficult times to bring us to Him to show us how real He is; and what He can do for us thru all that is going on. Many of these things, even if they are unpleasant at the time, are preparing us for what is ahead. So the next time you face an obstacle in your life run to Jesus. He will be standing there with open arms.

GET UNPACKED 214

When I was young I remember us getting big snowfalls keeping us from going to school. I remember one time when we had a big snowfall and it was about to thaw, another big snow fell on top of it. That happened several times packing the snow down making it hard to thaw. A lot of times life can bring things along our way that will make us feel "snowed under" or "packed down". I believe God wants us to give them all to Him. When we take this action, it's then we feel the weight lifted and it is as if we have been "unpacked" by God's love and His presence.

I DON'T WANT TO HEAR IT

We used to have four Pomeranians who used to sleep with us. We would go to bed and the dogs would begin "arguing" with each other. I remember Mike would say in a gentle voice "I don't want to hear it" and they would settle down and become quiet. One night I went to bed before my husband and the dogs started fussing. I told them to be quiet; settle down and I didn't want to hear it; but without success. But then I had an idea. I told them "Mike doesn't want to hear it" and that did the trick. When the enemy comes to you with lies- just tell him "I don't want to hear it". He has to go.

NOT MY WILL

If we look at our life, what changes could we make to make our life better? What new commitments can we make? As Christians we must put "self" away and seek God's guidance. What do I mean by "self". Our "self will" must be replaced by His will. Our entire life must be totally centered around Christ. We must allow God to change our heart; our thinking; our desires and our plans. When we are willing to let this happen; our entire life will become more enjoyable; just knowing God is in control of our life; and not us. We must always pray "Lord not my will, but thine be done".

DUCKS IN A ROW

I love watching ducks on a pond. I've watched as they line up in a straight line and swim across the water. It is a beautiful sight. I wonder if we have all "our ducks in a row". What does that mean? We must have all our priorities in a correct pattern. I would hope the things of God would be at the top of the list; and everything else underneath it. If we use this format, then our life will be so much easier and life will be worth living. Without Christ at the top, our life can become chaos. This year lets make sure we have everything centered around Christ.

TRUE FRIENDSHIP 218

Years ago I made what is called "Friendship Bread". It was very delicious. You had to have a "starter" to make this bread; but the neat thing about this bread you could make a variety of flavors. That's a lot like friends. My husband and I treasure the "variety" of friends we have made over the years. We feel everyone needs some good friends in their life. There are many people out there looking for a true friend. One to be there in the rough times as well as the good times; and a friend that will show them they care. Just as the Friendship Bread needs a "starter"; so we can be the one that "starts" a new friendship in the life of someone today.

A SONG MAKES A DIFFERENCE 219

Growing up I remember hearing my mom singing while cleaning the house or cooking. One of those songs was "Turn Your Radio On". Many times I have turned my radio on and a song playing has spoken to my heart or lifted my spirits. It seemed it was just the song I needed to hear for whatever I was going thru in my life. If you are going thru a hard time in your life just "turn your eyes upon Jesus. Look full in His wonderful face. And the things of this earth will grow strangely dim, in the light of His Glory and Grace". Keep a song in your heart. It will make a big difference in your life.

WHO'S IN CONTROL? 220

Our world often-times seems really disturbed. Many people will become discouraged or fearful with all the chaos and everything going on. I have found much hope in the fact that God is still in control; regardless of what is going on. I'm thankful we serve a big God…big enough to hold this entire universe in His hands; yet small enough to live in the heart of man. Our hope is not in man; but in Jesus Christ. We must not be afraid or run and hide. He said "Be not afraid-I am thy God". Enjoy this day because our anchor-Jesus-holds us in the palm of His hand and He is in control.

NO STRUGGLE 221

When we got saved, we were never promised a life without pain or bumps along the journey. We all love the good times; the "easy sailing" and when everything is going great. But those times that aren't very pleasant can draw us closer in our relationship with God. I like the quote that says "we experience just enough encouragement in life to keep us on our feet; yet enough discouragement to keep us on our knees". We all want to be on our feet; but it's equally as important to be on our knees. That's the way we can get thru life without a struggle.

MEASURING UP

When I was young I went into hardware stores with dad. They would give away wall calendars and yard-sticks. My mom used the yardsticks in the house and my dad would use them in the wood shed when he would be building things. It seems people use measuring tapes now instead of the yardsticks. Some parents measure their children's height to see how much they've grown in over a certain period of time. Have we grown in our relationship with God? Do we "measure up" in our attitude; our time used or our faith? Let's not fall "short" in these areas; but "measure up" in God's eyes.

May we all grow on this journey with the Lord.

THE DESIGN OF A QUILT

Many ladies get together to have a quilting club. Our neighbor before she passed away, would bring down her quilting bin every winter to make quilts for her family. I loved to see all the designs of her quilts. I have always liked quilts…bought or homemade. Every stitch represents someone's special touch. Most of the squares are from clothing from someone's past. We are a lot like a quilt. We represent tears; pain; joy and happiness over the years. When one stitch on a quilt is pulled loose-the connection is not as tight. So are we. Together we make a powerful difference in others.

THE RIGHT TEMPERATURE

I cook a lot of my meals in the microwave and the crock-pot. It's very rare that I use our range or oven; unless I am baking or making bread. I actually like using both of these ways of cooking. The crockpot cooks food slow and tenderizes the food; yet the microwave cooks from the inside-out; and is much faster. So it is with our life. God has changed us from the inside-out; very quickly. But sometimes He brings His plan to us at a "slow" process; tenderizing our heart. He knows what He is doing and what is best for each of us. Don't accept a "hot-oven" offer-when God has a much better method awaiting you.

SUCCESS AND FAILURE　225

Each of us have been blessed over the years. As we look over our lives we can see how faithful God has been. Any success we have had is because of God's grace. We may feel we have failed in our walk with God; but God doesn't see it that way. I heard a saying that really stuck with me. "Never let success get to your head; and never let failure get to your heart". That means never take credit for what we have accomplished; and never let failure hinder us from reaching our goals in life. Man views success different from God. Success is what God sees in us-not what man sees. I would say that's all that really matters anyway.

A LEAP OF FAITH　226

As a teenager I had an orange colored cat I called Pumpkin. One day after a big snowfall, I let her outside. I heard her meowing over and over. I looked and she was up in a tree. I went over stretched my hand up to her and she reached her paw down to me; but we could never connect. I kept thinking "how will I ever get her down"? Finally she took a leap down out of the tree. That's a lot like us when we are facing a situation in our life. It feels our faith will not reach far enough to grasp the answer. But all God is asking is for us to take a leap of faith. It is then we realize it wasn't has hard as we thought it would be.

THE GOOD NEWS 227

I recall going downtown as a child with my dad and seeing young men walking up and down the streets carrying the local newspaper. I remember hearing them shout "Newspaper newspaper. Get your newspaper". They had the local news of our city for anyone who wanted it. A minister in our town would hold a sign out his car window reading JESUS. He wanted to share the great news with others. We find it easy to share news of a new baby, a wedding; a new house, car or truck or a new job. But sometimes we find it hard to share our faith. It is so important we share the best news ever -Jesus. Our world could really use a little good news.

COLLECTING OUR THOUGHTS 228

Most of us have collected items over the years. My husband's aunt collected salt and pepper shakers. I've been fascinated with "old" drinking glasses. I have a nice collection; some may be valuable, even though I didn't pay much for them. Spiritually we need to collect our thoughts; doing an inventory of each thought we have. Philippians 4:8 says to think on things that are "true, just, honest, pure, lovely or good report". Our prayer should be "Lord let our minds stay on you-so you won't have to constantly be cleaning it up."

A QUICK FIX

I recall coming home from school; and as I walked into the house I could smell fresh homemade yeast rolls baking in the oven. It took most of the day for my mom to get the dough ready to rise and then bake. It wasn't a "quick-fix" at all. In life we aren't a "quick-fix" either. In fact God's still working on us. Romans 7:21 says "when I would do good-evil is present with me". That means we "knead" God to work in our life daily so we can "rise" up and do the things He wants us to do. Our life can be a sweet "aroma" to bring others to Christ.

←————————————→

A LAUGH, SONG AND WHISTLE

I recall growing up hearing men whistle or laugh as they worked. Everyone was happy, even though life was hard. It seems people aren't really happy today-you can hear it in their voice. It's a proven fact that things won't bring true happiness; and neither will money. Someone asked Rockefeller how much money it would take to make a person happy. His reply was "just a little bit more". Many people are not satisfied because they are looking for joy in the wrong things. Only the things of God will bring you true happiness. When you can smile thru a storm in your life-that's called JOY. That's the only thing that will make you laugh, sing and whistle.

←————————————→

BY AND BY

Our dog loves to go bye-bye. When getting ready to go somewhere, she stares at me as if she is asking if she can go too. When I tell her "I will be right back" she runs to get in my husband's lap. I think that means he won't go without her knowing it. It reminds me of a song we used to sing in church "By and by when the morning comes". This song was written by Charles Tindley a Methodist preacher. When he was two years old his mother passed away. After that time he became a "hired-worker". Life wasn't easy for him, but he knew one day he would "understand it better by and by". So will you and I…so will we.

EXERCISE DAILY 232

My sister and I take daily walks as often as possible. When the weather turns cold, we have to watch for days we can exercise. It would be easy to just stay in and wait for Spring. But we push forward and take every opportunity possible. In our walk with the Lord, we must exercise our spiritual man as well. During the day, many interruptions will occur; but it is up to each of us to make every effort to exercise our "walk" with God and faith by daily prayer and devotions. That is the best way for each of us to stay "strong and fit" in our daily "walk" with God.

ON-HOLD 233

When our little dog goes out, we give her a treat when she comes back in. She will stare at us and won't let us forget. I smile when we give the treat to her and she walks around holding it in her mouth. She waits before she chews and swallows it. A lot of times, we as Christians, are guilty of this. God "treats" us with blessings; but lots of times we put them "on-hold" never partaking of them. As long as we just hold on to it-we can never benefit from it. I believe He wants us to "chew it" and "swallow it". Remember God doesn't wait until we do something good; He "daily loadeth us with benefits". Psalms 68:19.

SHOWING LOVE   234

Everyone needs to feel loved. People will say they love you, but some don't show it. A story is told of a couple with their little girl at a restaurant. The little one kept waving at a man across the room who was dirty and wearing shaggy clothes. The mother was embarrassed; afraid others would see. As they left and passed the man, the little girl reached out and hugged the man. Tears coming down his face, the man looked at the mom and said "thank you ma'am. That's the first hug I have had in many years." That little girl taught her mom a lesson. Yes, the greatest is LOVE.

THE DEW FROM HEAVEN   235

I make a dessert called Apple-Dews. It is a lot like Apple Dumplins. You wrap your apple slices with crescent rolls and place in an oblong pan. You then melt some butter mixed with sugar and cinnamon and pour over the apple-crescent. Next you pour a can of Mountain Dew over that and bake. The Mountain Dew adds the final touch. It reminds me how a dew will fall overnight causing the bushes and grass to glisten in the sunlight. In our life, the dew represents the Holy Spirit fallen over us. The "SON" shines down on us causing our life to glow and radiate to others.

CLEARING THE RUBBISH   236

I go out and sit on the porch in the morning while our little dog is in the yard. I was looking across our yard when I saw some twigs, limbs and debris laying on the yard. I knew they needed to be picked up so when the green grass begins to come up, it could be seen better. As Christians we must be careful that "debris" does not show up in our life. We want to make sure we keep our life clean and spotless before Him. Like our yard, we must remove all pride; unforgiveness; and selfish desires so God's love can shine thru for others to see. It will get the attention of many that come our way.

$$\longleftrightarrow$$

FITTING IN   237

As a young girl my heart would go out to students who looked lonely or didn't fit-in. I always tried to be friendly to them, because that was the way I was taught. The older I get, the more I realize things haven't really changed. There are those who feel neglected, left out and not a part of a "group". I am so glad that God doesn't look at man the way people do. Doesn't matter where we come from; whether we are rich or poor; young or old; short or tall....God loves us. Giving our heart to Jesus makes us a Kings Kid. What more could we ask for to "fit in" in God's family?

$$\longleftrightarrow$$

ON FIRE   238

Growing up in the country I remember hearing the wind whistling thru the trees. I could tell it was getting cold. Sometimes my dad would say "I believe it is blowing in a snow".

My dad kept plenty of wood in the fire so our home would be warm. The older I get, the more I don't like freezing cold weather. As Christians, when we become "cold" in our walk with God, we will become miserable. It's then we don't feel the presence of the Lord like before. We must make sure the "fire" doesn't go out. We must allow the Holy Spirit to continue to "burn" in our heart. The closer we get to God, the more "on-fire" we will become.

NO TIME FOR FLIP FLOPS 239

When I was young, most children played outside bare-foot. I remember wearing flip-flops all summer until they were worn out and thin. In life we find people that are "flip-floppy" and "wishy-washy". That means they don't keep their promises, their word; or deals they make. Some don't go thru with what they say or promise. They go back on their word. As a Christian we must "practice what we preach". There is no time for a "flip-floppy" or "wishy-washy" Christian. People need to see the "real thing". That's the only way we can win them to the Lord.

HE'S GOT OUR BACK 240

We go to the park and watch the ducks swimming across the pond. I read where ducks feathers are coated with an oily substance from a gland in their body. That's where the saying "rolls off like water on a duck's back" came from. When people use this saying, they are meaning that things said or done don't bother them; they let things "roll" right off their back. When things occur in our life, it's best we just "let go" of it so we can get over it and not let it disturb our life. Only God can help us to move forward. Think about the oil on the ducks back and remember God's got our back and He's handling it all anyway.

TAKE A LOOK 241

As a little girl my dad would buy me a box of animal crackers. I enjoyed them and especially eating them. You can still buy them-but something is different about them. My dad bought them for five cents a box. Now they are more than that. I never took the box and put them up and just looked at it. You see if I had never opened the box I would have never seen the animals or enjoyed the taste. God has so many gifts of blessings for us; but we never open those gifts. It is up to us to open the box. When we get it opened we should look for the gift of His love, presence, peace and joy and enjoy each day in spite of what we may go thru. We are blessed!

OFF THE BEATEN PATH 242

We've heard the saying "off the beaten path". Many of us were raised "off the beaten path". My husband and I have found some of those roads on our trips. That's a road not traveled a lot; and not easily traveled. I prefer roads that are traveled a lot. Most people prefer the Interstate or six lane roads, over those narrow country roads. On our road to Heaven Matthew 7:14 explains that "narrow is the way that leads to life…few there be that find it". The narrow road may be less traveled; but I can assure you, it will lead us home. Maybe we should ask ourselves "what road am I on?" It's your choice.

KEEP ON DREAMING

Each of us have dreams; some good and some not so good. Also there are times we find ourselves day-dreaming. You can look in a person's face and see it in the "staring into space" look. It's as if their minds are thousands of miles away. I always dreamed I would go to Hawaii; but never thought it would come to pass. However, God made it possible for us to go twice. God gives each of us dreams for our life. If you have a dream and it hasn't come to pass…don't give up. His timing is perfect. Just keep on dreaming; but make sure it lines up to God's will for you.

NO "TRADING"

When I was a young girl going downtown with my dad, I recall seeing men sitting on benches at the Courthouse selling and trading knives and guns. On one occasion my dad traded his knife for another one a man had that day. Going home I remember dad told me he wished he had not traded it. As Christians many times the devil offers us "things" he makes look good; but are not worth trading for. When we became a Christian we traded sin for life; fear for faith; sadness for joy and a "past" for a "future". This life has too many benefits to trade. So the next time the enemy offers you a trade, be sure you reply "no deal".

TO WIN THE GAME

As a teenager-our family played the board game called Scrabble. Players had "letter pieces" they used to make a word. After all pieces were used and no one could form a word-the game was over. I tried to make up words to be the winner and add "fun" to the game. Have you ever noticed there are those who always want to have "the last word" even if it cost a friendship. I remember the words "a soft answer turneth away wrath". Many will "perceive" what someone else is thinking when really they aren't thinking it at all. None of us can read another person's mind. I've learned if we "live peacefully with all men" then we all win!

IN GOD'S HAND 246

We had beagles when I was young since my dad was a rabbit and squirrel hunter. But I remember there was a squirrel my dad would feed. It would sit on the limb watching for my dad to come outside. When dad walked over to the tree, the squirrel would come down and eat from my dad's hand. In reality God has blessings for us in His hand. He is waiting for us to come and reach out for it. It is as if He is saying "here it is-come and get it". It's up to us to make the move. Psalms 145:16 says it well "thou openest thine hand and satisfiest the desire of every living thing". Yes He does!

COLOR-COATED 247

Growing up we always had chickens and roosters. We never ran out of eggs, and when we wanted fried chicken we never had to go far. The rooster was our alarm clock. We would go to the feed store to buy little chicks. I remember walking in there and I could hear them in the back of the store. Near Easter they would have "colored" chicks; but those little chicks were sold for a higher price. I remember when "sin was sin"; but today sin is color-coated to make it more appealing for all ages; and not appearing as bad as it really is. Don't fall for the devil's schemes. It could "cost you more than you want to pay".

RUBBED THE WRONG WAY 248

The personality of a cat is different from a dog. A cat says "what can you do for me?" while a dog thinks "what can I do for you?" A cat doesn't like for you to rub their hair the wrong way. In fact they can get fighting mad. I've heard people say "that person rubs my hair the wrong way". What they mean is that person really gets on my nerves or irritates me. Life is too short to let people get on your nerves. A minister one time said "if a person rubs you the wrong way; turn around the opposite way and it won't bother you". That's pretty good advice.

DOWN MEMORY LANE 249

My sister and I drove down to the Cave where my dad worked years ago. There's a lot of memories there. I looked in the trees where a cabin stood at one time. Inside that cabin I was born-their third daughter. I looked down a path that led to the cave. I wondered how many steps my dad had walked down that path to give cave tours. I remember the day I was "born again". I wonder how many steps the Lord and I have walked together. We've walked together many years; side by side. Today reflect on where you came from and where you are today. You won't regret it.

IT'S NOT OVER 'TIL IT'S OVER

I've heard the saying "it's like riding a bike. You never forget how to ride it". I haven't ridden a bike in a long time; so I wonder if I still can. When I had a bicycle with training wheels as a young girl, I wasn't afraid of falling off; but a big bike was different. I fell off a few times; got some scratches and felt some hurt. In life we've all experienced some hurt and scratches; even fell down a few times; but the good thing is we got back up because the race wasn't over. Friend if this describes you, I encourage you to just hang on. God sees your faithfulness; and it is not over until He says "it's over".

I'M SORRY

There are so many words that are important to use. I think about "I love you" or "I'm here for you" plus many more. There is a couple of words I feel are neglected a lot. The words "I'm sorry" are not used enough. In our world today there are people that seem to take pleasure in hurting others. I was taught to make sure things were right between me and others. Today if someone has hurt you, why not make the first move. That's the heart of Jesus. His words were "Father forgive them for they don't know what they do." He forgave first and we can too.

NO SHOVELING

Many times we will hear snow mentioned in the forecast. My husband reminds me of a weather man several years ago who gave a forecast of 5-percent chance of snow for our area. The next morning a big snow was on the ground. A listener called in and asked that the guy who did the forecast the night before come and shovel his 5-percent snow. In life, sometimes we will feel we are "snowed under" with bills, problems and cares of life. Only God can "dig" you out of it all with no shoveling necessary. All we need is His love and His hand extended to us. We can experience it like the old hymn says "Love lifted me".

STARTING AND FINISHING 253

The church I attended almost twenty-five years began in a store-front building. God gave a vision to a man out of state to come and begin this work. Many said it would not work, but what began as a humble-beginning led to three sanctuaries. Hundreds walked thru that door including me and hundreds found the Lord to be their Savior. You see, it doesn't matter what side of the tracks we are from; God chose you and me to serve Him. He isn't finished with us because He has other stages of our life we have not possessed yet. Always remember…it's not how we got started; but how we finish this journey.

MAKING PREPARATIONS 254

One of my first jobs as a teenager was working at a donut shop. The owners went in real early to prepare the donuts and get them all cooked. It was my job to go in afterwards to fill the donuts and ice them to sell during the day. The preparation they did early made it easy for me to do my job. Jesus has gone away to prepare for our entrance into Heaven. St John 14:2 says "I go to prepare a place for you…..that where I am, there ye may be also". I believe the preparation is about over. If you ask me, that means we are almost "outta" here.

WATCH YOUR STEP

ICE! I had rather have snow any day. Ice is pretty but can be dangerous. When I was young we had cold temperatures with icicles hanging off the roof of our porch. When walking you can easily lose your footage on icy pavement and cause injury to your body. One car on ice in Texas caused a 133 car pile-up. That's the way it is in our life. One bad decision can affect not just ourselves; but our family and many others. We should walk this walk very carefully for others to follow. One wrong move or one wrong step can cause a dear friend to lose their footage.

THE OPEN DOOR

As a teen I applied for a job at a store near where we lived. I had no experience, but I decided to take the risk and apply. When I was hired for a position I felt it was an open door for me. I've had several doors open for me over the years. We must watch for doors that God opens for us; but we should also ask Him to close doors that are not His will for us. The important door to open is found in Rev 3:20 "behold I stand at the door and knock; if any man hear my voice and open the door, I will come in…I will sup with him and he with me". That open door will change your life completely. Be willing to let Him in.

A MANY SPLENDORED THING

"Love Is A Many Splendored Thing" was a song made famous years ago. It is saying that love is the greatest component anyone can experience. How true that is! Love is the greatest. Love can heal a broken heart and cover a multitude of sins. God loved us so much He gave His best. The old hymn says "The love of God is greater far than tongue or pen can ever tell. It goes beyond the highest star…and reaches to the lowest hell". The awesome thing about it is He loves us all. His words to all of us are "I will always love you". What more can you and I ask for?

THE SUN SHINING THRU 258

While growing up I remember a lot of heavy snows that came where we lived. Limbs would break under the pressure; and little snowbirds would search for food above that snow. Mom would throw bread crumbs out for them to eat. The sun would come out and glisten across the snow as it began to melt. There are many people today that feel they are about to break under the pressure they are going thru. Like the little birds, many people hunger and are looking for the bread of life. In the midst of your situation, I can tell you the Son will shine again and melt all your problems away; and provide what you need.

SAFE AND SECURE 259

When I was young I remember us going to church one night and coming outside when the service was over. The snow was really coming down and the ground was covered. When we got home the snow was so deep my dad picked me up and stood me on a stump. Isn't that like our heavenly Father? When we feel we are about to "sink" under the pressure, problems and cares of this life; our Savior comes and picks us up and places us in a safer place. Deut 33:12 says "the beloved of the Lord shall dwell in safety by Him". That's a comforting thought, isn't it?

SHARE YOUR STORY 260

Our life is like a story that can minister to others. A lot of personal experiences we encounter in our lifetime are worth being shared with others. Those experiences can inspire others; and may just be what someone needs to hear today. Each moment in our life can reflect the goodness of the Lord and there are many who need to hear of His faithfulness in our life. Our life is like a book and when it is opened and read by others, it can bring encouragement and peace to them, They can see the goodness of the Lord all along. It is true we have come this far by faith; and by faith we will continue on.

WHAT A VIEW 261

Years ago my husband, his parents and I went to St Louis, MO. We rode the arch up to the top. We climbed into what felt like a tunnel. They say it's like riding one-half Ferris wheel and one-half elevator. We went up 630 feet in 4 minutes. At the top we saw a view that was wonderful. I couldn't help but think this doesn't compare to the day when Jesus comes back for His children. Nothing will hold us back as a child of God. It will be a ride "out of this world". I believe we will be shouting "good-bye world; good-bye". What a ride and what a view awaits us.

THE BRIDE OF CHRIST 262

It's an amazing story how God brought my husband and I together. I remember the day I was preparing to walk the isle to be my husband's bride. I wanted to look my best for him; no spots and dirt on my wedding dress. I carried a small white

Bible he had given to me, covered in white satin and white roses. We had no doubt, we knew God had put us together. John tells about the new city coming down from Heaven prepared as a bride adorned for her husband. Christ is coming back for those who are looking for His return; without spot or wrinkle. Who knows, it could be today.

NO LACK WITH GOD 263

My husband and I went to Hawaii twice; a dream come true. I always wanted to go and God made it possible. There was a revolving restaurant that we wanted to go to; but felt it would be too expensive. We talked about it and decided to wait until the last day to go. When we went, we found out it was very reasonable and the food was great. We looked at each other thinking we could have already eaten there several times. That's a lot like our walk with God. We are afraid it will "cost too much" if we proceed to do what God has called us to do. But I have found out, when God arranges a plan for us, there is no lack with God.

LOOK FOR IT! 264

My sisters, parents and I would go to the garden in the late afternoon after it cooled off to gather vegetables. I recall one time while picking veggies, my dad saw a cloud coming up and told us we had better get home. I looked and saw something very interesting. In the distance you could see the rain coming down in sheets; but where we were it wasn't raining yet. As Christians, if we don't see it, it's hard to believe it's coming. But God sees what we don't see. We must believe God because He promised there would be Showers of Blessings! And they are on your way.

———————→

WE MUST BE READY   265

I remember Sept 11, 2001 very well. We were in Colorado visiting my husband's family. That day got the attention of all the people. Eyes were glued to the TV. Many prayed who had not prayed in a long time. God is trying to get the attention of people today. He's saying time is running out. Today is the day of salvation. The saddest thing is thinking of being left behind when Jesus comes back. It will be chaos everywhere. Once again people will be watching the news; praying and crying out to God. The best thing is to make sure we are ready today.

———————→

WEIGHT-LIFTER   266

Mike and I have had the opportunity to fly a few times. It is an experience you won't ever forget. You can feel the anticipation of the passengers as the plane begins to lift off. As you fly higher and higher into the sky, everything below becomes so tiny in your sight. As you go beyond the clouds, it's a feeling you cannot describe. It seems as if you left everything behind. God wants to lift you and me above our troubles, worries, cares and concerns. He is really good at lifting our spirits and bringing joy back into our life. I would say He is the best "weight-lifter" you and I could ever meet.

TO MOVE FORWARD

When we look around there are so many changes occurring in our town. Our city is working on building a new Arena in the downtown area. Some buildings had to be demolished to make room for this structure. But one day there will be a brand new building standing there. In our life, there are things that need to be destroyed to move forward in our walk with the Lord. Some things we may not want to "let go of". God wants to do a "new thing" in our walk with Him if we will allow Him to. When we "tear down" those walls, it's exciting to see what God has in store. We can then move forward.

ANOTHER MAN'S SHOES

Have you ever known someone that judged a person by their first appearance? We've heard the saying "don't judge me until you've walked a mile in my shoes". People will give advice, offer their opinion or say "if that was me I would do it this way, not that way". We really don't know what we would do until we are in that position. Sometimes it's good to "step" into the shoes of others to feel real compassion for them. I believe our opinion and thinking will change and our lives will be totally blessed. That's what it feels like to walk in another man's shoes.

CALL YOUR ORDER IN

When my husband and I were dating, we would go to a drive-up restaurant that had curb-service. Mike had an eight-track player, so we would listen to music and talk. We would call our food order in and watch as cars drove around and around as if they had nothing else to do. It was interesting to watch. That's a lot like people today. They are going around in circles; with no clarity of what they want in life. They can't find what they are looking for. If you feel that way today, just look to God. He is waiting for you to "call your order in". He has everything and anything you need.

TEAR DROPS 270

When I was young my sisters and I used to sing together as a trio in churches. My older sister played the guitar for us. One song we would sing was "He Washed My Eyes With Tears". People with tears in their eyes will ask me to forgive them for crying; but I always tell them God created tears for a reason. Even Jesus wept when His good friend passed away. Tears will bring a release in our spirit, heart and from all our hurt. Don't be ashamed of your tears because "Tears are a language God Understands". Always remember "weeping may endure for a night; but joy comes in the morning".

ALL IN A PICTURE 271

I went to the same elementary school for eight years. Every year each class would have a group picture taken. As the years went by you could see the difference in our appearance. Some of us had different hairstyles, or had gotten taller. As Christians we can look back and see a difference over the years as well; hopefully for the better. We should have grown more in the Lord. Our countenance should show God's love and grace; as well as the radiance of the Holy Spirit reflecting from our life. Each of us should have grown and gotten more "mature" as we walked this walk with God.

A LITTLE FRESH AIR

As a little girl I remember waking up and hearing my mom washing clothes using a wringer washing machine. After they washed she would take them outside and hang them on the clothesline to dry in the fresh air. Times were not as easy then; but my mom enjoyed being a housewife and mom because she was doing it for those she loved…her family. It's the same way with us on our journey to Heaven. Life can be complex; but we can enjoy it because of the one we serve. As cares arise, hang them on the "clothes-line" of life. The breath of the Holy Spirit will take care of the rest.

←——————————→

A FULL MENU

273

There's a restaurant on the river in Ashland City, TN I love to go to. I always order the whole catfish. It is served with two catfish and is so delicious. Just ask anyone who goes with us and they will tell you I clean it to the bones. That's because when I go I make sure I am hungry and have a good appetite. I don't eat a lot of snacks or junk food before going. In our walk with the Lord, we must have a good appetite for the things of God. There is so many blessings God wants to give each of us. Junk and things of this world will not fulfill that hunger. Today go to God's table and feast. He bids "come and dine".

←——————————→

SOMETHING BETTER

274

I remember my dad and my two sisters going to town one day. I always wanted to go; but for some reason that day I chose to stay home. After they left I started crying wishing I had gone with them. I cried and cried. Mom told me as soon as she was finished in the kitchen, she would get the Sears catalog and we would cut out paper dolls. She knew how to calm me down and get my mind off of not going. When we are sad or disappointed in life, our Heavenly Father comes along and calms all our sadness by wiping the tears away. Whatever caused us disappointment, He always offers something better. That's just the way He is.

OF MORE VALUE 275

As a teen, I remember we got an aluminum tree with a color wheel. I loved looking at it. I thought is was so different from a regular tree. I would like to have one now; but they are scarce and hard to find because they are of much more value now. As Christians we are a treasure to our Heavenly Father. As that color wheel brought beauty to the tree with its lights; so does the Holy Spirit shine His light on us, so others can see the Glory of God radiating on our life. You see we aren't like those who are in the world. We are different because of Him. You are so valuable to God; because God doesn't make junk.

NEVER GROW OLD 276

I use my cell phone a lot every day. Most people have a smart phone; but mine is a "dumb phone" because it is a flip-phone. Some of us older folk like those. A couple of features aren't working right. I have problems retrieving group messages and pictures. Its good to know we have no problem retrieving messages from God; and the things of God never grow old either. Things grow old and each of us are growing older; but when we get to Heaven we will be "In A Land Where We Will Never Grow Old". The good thing is cell phones won't be needed there either.

BROKEN FENCES 277

I saw on TV where a man's fences had gotten broken down and his animals were scattered. He looked but it was difficult to locate and bring them home. After he found them the owner had his fence repaired immediately. That's like a person's life. Words spoken or harbored feelings can cause "broken fences" in relationships that are hard to mend if we wait too long. This can hinder our walk with God and our testimony. Let's make sure we repair the "broken fences' and make things right. We never know when we may have to go back to that fence again.

GOING THE EXTRA MILE 278

My dad's nephew had a bad drinking problem. One day he stopped by our house after drinking. My dad did not turn him away; but talked to him about the Lord and gave him scriptures. I remember my mom cooking a special meal for him to eat with us. Most people would have turned him away; but my parents did what they should do…show the love of Jesus to him. There are those who feel forsaken or rejected because of choices they have made. They need to see Jesus in us. Let's go the extra mile to win them to God.

AMAZING

I remember going with our church teen group to Mammoth Cave. Our bus driver planned the trip so well. Halfway thru the tour we stopped at an area that had tables and chairs where we could eat our sack lunches we had brought with us. Fifty years later I still remember the excitement of that trip as a teenager. Looking back we can view wonderful experiences we've had on this Christian journey. Like the cave tour it was long and we got tired; but the joy of the experience was much greater. Our walk with the Lord had its ups and down, but it's been an amazing journey, don't you think?

ALL IS CALM

After my dad passed away, our family moved from the country to the city. It was a big change for us from what we were used to. In the country all was quiet. We saw the stars and the moon at night; but in the city, we saw street lights and heard the sound of traffic. In the city in the middle of the night I had to get used to the sound of the train; but it wasn't long before I had gotten used to it. Let's be careful that things that are unpleasing to God don't creep into our lives and we get "used to it". It must disturb us enough that we want no part of it. When we do that, all is calm and peaceful.

A PRICELESS POSSESSION

Many of us have started projects, with good intentions of finishing it. Before long we have put them away, but we never find ourselves going back to it. Some of the items may have just needed a little touch-up or a little paint to make it beautiful again. I'm glad God doesn't put us away and lose interest in doing some "repairs' on us. We all could use a little "touch-up" job, because we aren't the finished product yet. God is still working on you and me. But when He is finished, we will be a priceless possession for him.

THE PRIZE INSIDE 282

I loved buying a box of candy when I was a small girl especially if it had a prize inside of it. Inside each of us is a prize God has created when we became a child of God. We are a light for a dark world. We hold the key to joy and peace and the love that everyone is looking for. But the great prize comes when we get to Heaven. Philippians 3:14 says "I press toward the mark, for the prize of the high calling of God in Christ Jesus". Isn't that exciting? It's something we can all look forward to.

NEVER LEAVE HIS PRESENCE 283

Going to Beech Bend park was an exciting trip for our family. The cost to get in was a whopping ten cents. We would ride the rides; go to the petting zoo and visit all the gift shops. We would spend the entire day; and when it was time to go, no one wanted to leave. We didn't want it to end. Things in life are like that. Nothing stays forever. But some things never fade away. God's love, His grace, and His mercy will always be there. I'm glad for the promise where He said He would never leave us. I have the same feeling we had when we left Beech Bend park. I don't want to ever leave God's presence.

DON'T FALL THRU 284

After our pastors left Clarksville, they went to Gun Barrel City, Texas. My husband and I decided to go on a trip there and surprise them. We spent the night in a motel there and wanted to get up the next morning and go to their church to surprise them. We walked into the motel and there was a chair with a cushion in it. When I sat down, I fell completely thru. There was no webbing in the chair. A Good laugh with no injuries. In life the devil will make things look appealing; but those offers always fall thru. We must stay away from his schemes so we won't get badly hurt.

DUMPED ON 285

I have a cake recipe I've made in the past that is so moist. It's called Dump-Cake. Each item is dumped into the greased pan and then it is baked. It's amazing how the items come together and make a sweet dessert without mixing it together. In life you may feel you have been "dumped on". Your life seems like a disaster and will never come together. But it's great to know God can take all of that and make an amazing blessing out of all the "mess". Don't worry what it looks like and appears to be. In fact our life becomes a sweet fragrance of His Holy Spirit when others come around.

A HEART OF PRAISE 286

When I was a teenager, we had an awesome song leader in our church. He was the most excited person I had ever met. I believe he could feel the Spirit in every bone he possessed.

His enthusiasm was extended into the congregation. People would enter in and worship the Lord together because it was real. Many have lost that zeal and excitement with the Lord; therefore the praise is not there anymore. But when we praise Him, things begin to happen. God can work thru those who praise Him. Let's come back to a heart of worship and praise to God.

MORE THAN A NOBODY 287

The story tells of a work that was needing to be done in a church. It was put "on hold" because "somebody" was waiting for "anybody" to do it. So it never got done because "nobody" would do it. There are things that need to be done to win the lost to Christ. Souls are dying while we wait for another person to win them to the Lord. But "somebody" has to do it. Most people are saying 'anybody' can do that better than me. But nobody does it, so souls are dying and not getting right with God. Let's be the "somebody" and "step up to the plate" and begin the work. I've found out, others will follow too.

STAND UP 288

I loved going to Opryland theme park over the years until it was closed. We were there one time when the Kingsmen Quartet did a live taping in the park. That was so exciting. One song had the words "stand up" in it. Every time they said those words in the song, they wanted the audience to stand up. There was so much excitement as everyone stood and shouted "stand up". I believe God wants us to be brave and stand up for what is right. We must let others know we are not ashamed of the gospel; and we are happy to stand up for Jesus!

BEING A FRIEND

We have a great niece who is 14 years old. She is so special.
She always has a smile; very pleasant; loving and so sensitive
to the feelings of others. Her disposition reminds me of God.
He is sensitive to all our needs and wants us to be kind to
others. There is a saying that says "you can attract more bees
with honey than with vinegar". That means we can gain more
friends by being kind; and more people to Christ by showing
God's love. A friend loveth at all times. Now is a good time for
us to give someone a smile. Who knows we may just gain a new
friend.

←———————————→

THE "CONE" OF GOD'S WILL

As a kid I loved getting cotton candy. I was fascinated watching
it spin around in the bin and being put on a cone. I always
wanted a pink one even though there were other colors to
choose from. As a "big kid" I still enjoy cotton candy. It will
melt and disappear very fast when you place it in your mouth.
If we aren't careful, our dreams and promises will disappear
quickly. We must grasp them tightly so they don't slip away.
When life is "spinning around" in circles, keep your focus on
Christ. They will come together and attach to the "cone" of
God's will at the right time for you to enjoy them all.

←———————————→

SEARCH NO MORE

When my four nieces were young, we would hide Easter eggs
for them to hunt. We had a little Terrapoo who loved searching
for the eggs with them. It was funny watching her find an egg,

pick it up and lay it back down; then look for another one. In life there are people searching for something to fill the vacancy in their life. They are out there searching but can't find what is missing. They will purchase things and go places; but it doesn't satisfy that empty spot in their life. It can only be found in Jesus Christ. The old hymn says it well: "only Jesus will satisfy your soul". If you are on a "hunt" for something, look no farther. Turn to Jesus.

<hr>

WHAT A THRILL 292

The county fair has been an exciting event for families to attend for years with all the food; rides and other events. People have stood in long lines to ride "crazy rides". I've watched them go to the top and "zoom" down to the bottom at a high rate of speed; with loud screaming from the riders. Well, that's not for me. Spiritually each of us have had some "rides" in our lifetime. We've had our "highs and lows" and not all were a thrill. But we can all look back and declare "what an adventure and what a thrill" with God holding the controls.

<hr>

GOD'S PAINTING 293

Some people have a real knack for painting. I love to see paintings of old barns and country scenes. It brings back a lot of memories of living in the country as a child. But my favorite is mountain scenes. Famous artist have sold such paintings for thousands of dollars. But the best art is the paintings God puts in the sky of a sunset or sunrise. His artwork also includes the colors of mountains in every season. Only God can paint these moments. You can't really describe the majestic view. Not only is He the artist but the one that formed this view. These views are priceless!

SCRAMBLED 294

When I was young we would go to Ben Franklin Store downtown on Third street. It was there we would buy the best hamburgers you could find. They were scrambled and topped with grated cabbage. But the secret was the special sauce they used. They were unique in the flavor it produced. I've met a lot of people with their life "scrambled" or "confused" not sure what to do in their life. The Holy Spirit is that 'secret sauce' we need in our life to lead and direct our path. When He guides us, all the confusion leaves and peace will flood our soul. O taste & see He is good.

ALL IN A RUSH 295

When you are out on the highway, it's imperative you watch and be careful. It's hard to believe how fast people drive. They will fly right past you like you were sitting still. One friend said when someone is speeding "they drive like they stole it". People are always in a rush. A rush to go to work; a rush to go home; and a rush even in a fast-food drive-up. There are some things we cannot rush. For instance, we can't rush God's answers to our prayers. God knows what He is doing. Even if we think they are late; He is always on time. He's God and He knows what's best.

WORDS CAN'T EXPLAIN IT

Have you ever had great experiences in life you just couldn't explain? It seems words could not be found to describe it. Yet you can say it was a joyful moment in your life. That's the way it is with Christ and the things of God. It's hard to explain how you felt when you got saved or filled with the Holy Spirit. It's hard to explain the tokens of love He has bestowed on you. It's difficult to explain the miracles you have experienced in your life. Those who don't believe do not understand those feelings. One dear saint of God said it well when she said "it's better felt than telt". That means we can feel it but we just can't tell how it is.

A MESSAGE IN THE CLOUDS

My sister and I were walking thru the park and I looked up in the sky and saw the big fluffy clouds. There was a gold lining around one as the sun appeared from behind it. I thought about the saying that says "there will be a silver lining around the clouds". In your despair look for the silver lining. I also couldn't help but think about the day when Jesus steps out onto the clouds to come and gather His children. 1 Thessalonians 4:17 reads "they which are alive and remain shall be caught up together in the clouds…ever to be with the Lord". The next time you see clouds in the sky, just imagine our Savior there bidding us come.

THIRST-QUENCHER 298

I was sitting on our front porch watching our little dog. All of a sudden I saw five deer running across our neighbor's yard. Our little dog got so excited. They were the fastest "deer-doggies" she had seen. Psalms 42:1 says "as the hart "deer" panteth after the water brooks, so panteth my soul after thee O God". Deer are so happy when they come to a brook of water for a drink. You and I should want that living water Jesus gives like He did to the Samaritan woman at Jacob's well. He said "you will never thirst again". That's a great thirst-quencher".

⟷

IN HIS SHADOW 299

I remember as a young girl playing in our yard; and trying to step on my shadow. Every time I would step it moved. I also recall walking behind my dad and stepping into his shadow. You see it all depends on the position of the sun whether your shadow is in front of you, beside you, or behind you. If you are walking in the shadow of sin or an experience you've had in your life; try stepping out of those shadows, into the shadow of the SON. I guarantee it won't be as hard as you think it will be. As the song says "walking somewhere in the shadow you'll find Jesus." He cares and understands.

⟷

DON'T FEAR THE OBSTACLE 300

My husband and I went to Port Royal Bridge with our small dog. She was our first dog and loved to go places with us. Walking around the curve, our dog saw a parked motorcycle. She was so afraid of it and would not walk around it. One other time we went to Florida and brought two watermelons home with us. We put them in the corner of the far end of the kitchen. She was so afraid of them, she would walk the long way around to avoid them. That's a lot like Christians. Things that won't hurt them will terrify them. They allow things of life to scare them; but God has not given us a spirit of fear. His love will cast out all fear.

GIVING FLOWERS 301

I have always loved beautiful flowers; but don't really have a "green thumb". One day at work, my husband met an elderly couple that used to live near us when I was a child. They were good friends of my dad and they were always so nice to me. He told my husband I used to pick his flowers and sell them back to him for a quarter. I didn't remember that, but I did get a laugh from it. That reminded me how we should "give flowers" to people who have blessed us while they are alive…not expecting anything in return. These deeds will make us feel better and I know it pleases God as well.

UNWRAPPED 302

We got our first dog one week after we were married. We taught her so many tricks. Many times at night, my husband would hear me telling her to "roll over". She caught on very quickly. We had bought the orange and black wrapped peanut butter kisses and had them in a bowl on our coffee-table. When we came home that day, there were orange and black wrappers all over the floor; but the candy was gone. She met us at the door so happy. There are many blessings and gifts God has for us; but we are hesitate to unwrap them. Until we open each one, we will never know the joy they will bring to us. Open them today.

THE CLIMB 303

I love going to the mountains in East Tennessee. I can feel God's peace in such powerful ways. My sister and I decided to climb Clingsmans Dome. It was a long climb; but we made it to the top and saw all the beauty. Coming down was harder than I thought it would be. We decided to rest a moment. My foot was sitting in a puddle of water and I didn't even realize it. Both of us had to laugh. If we aren't careful we will become "numb" to the feelings of the things going on in our life. May we always stay alert and keep a watchful eye for things that may slip up on us that aren't best for us.

NO MORE RERUNS 304

Our widows and sponsors did a dinner-show for our church to raise funds for our widows. It was called TV Reruns. Each person acted out a TV character and even spoke a few lines from the character. They dressed like their TV star also. One of our sponsors was Fonz on Happy days. He rode in on his motorcycle. It was so much fun! In life people will do reruns of their past. But we are saved and forgiven from our sins and our past. I believe God is saying do not go back to those days. We don't need any reruns of how we used to be. I suggest what Paul said "forgetting those things which are behind us". Yes, no more reruns.

DON'T FEAR THE STORMS

Rain can bring floods and the closure of roads. When I was in elementary school a road close to our home flooded. The bus wasn't able to make our route. In 2010 a flood kept me from getting to work. I had tried every route but could not get there. We hear the saying "turn around-don't drown". Many people are flooded with problems, bills, tears, questions and emotions. I offer this to you. "Turn around-don't drown: give it all to God". Isaiah 59:19 says "when the enemy shall come in like a flood; the Spirit of the Lord shall lift up a standard against him". Jesus is our shelter.

HOW BEAUTIFUL IT IS

One week it's freezing; the next it's warm. That's what we call Tennessee weather. I can already see spurts of grass trying to come up. It's like they're saying the "cold" won't last forever… spring is coming and here I come. One day we will leave all pain, problems and sorrow behind. A new day will be dawning. A good friend used to sing a song called "Come Spring". It says "we'll meet when God gathers flowers, come spring". No beauty will compare with it there. "How Beautiful Heaven Must Be". A land of peace, joy and love. "Won't It Be Wonderful There" where "Roses will Bloom Again".

DON'T STAY DOWN

My husband and I live on a dead-end street. Vehicles come down and turn around in our driveway trying to go back up the street. Our mailbox got knocked down many times, making it hard for my husband to keep putting it up. But we got it moved close to our porch. My heart goes out to those who have been "put down" or "knocked down" in life. They feel they will never "fit-in". Moving the mailbox stopped the problem we were having. If you feel "down on yourself", move away from anyone or anything that "knocks you down" and run to Jesus who will "lift you up".

BEST DECISION EVER   308

Most of us have made many decisions in our life. Many decisions I made have impacted my life all these years. But in October 1967 I walked the isles of a church and knelt at an old-fashioned alter and gave everything to Christ. That was the best decision I have ever made. I was a changed teenager. If you are looking for a change in your life, I recommend you giving your heart, life, plans, and desires to Him. You will never regret it. You will feel completely different. "Behold old things will be passed away and all things will become new". Right where you are make that decision today.

A SNAIL'S PACE   309

On a rainy day, I love to go into the kitchen and make a soup in my crock-pot. I love to put all kinds of veggies and seasonings in it. I've found out the longer it cooks, the better it tastes. In life, sometimes we feel it takes a long time to get an answer or hear from God. But the longer we wait, the more we enjoy receiving the answer. It is flavored with God's spirit, love and joy. There is a reason He delays His answer. It is as if He knows just what we need and when we need it. I can assure you even if it comes at a snail's pace, it will come right on time. Don't give up.

A MELODY IN OUR HEART

310

I love good gospel singing. Lots of times the songs will just soothe my being. As a young girl I would hear my mom singing as she did her housework. Hearing her sing brought such joy to me when I was inside playing. Many times I have heard a song and it would minister to me as I listened to the words. Each of us need a melody in our heart to help us get thru the day or even the long night. I encourage you to ask God to put a melody in your spirit and you will discover how much of a difference it will make in your life.

←——————————→

FORGIVE TO BE FORGIVEN

311

Years ago when we would go to the Mountains a good friend would come and stay with our first little dog. She was so good to our dog. I often think when we arrived home, how our dog would meet us at the door so excited to see us. But in just a few minutes she would run and hide; upset that we had left her. My husband would have to go and apologize to her. It's funny how she would be ok after that apology. Many people remember what people have done to them and will not forgive. It's important that we have a forgiving heart. If we can't forgive, will God forgive us? We must forgive others to be forgiven by God.

←——————————→

MAKE A DIFFERENCE

312

I personally don't like suspension bridges. They don't feel safe to me when I am walking across them. Most of us want to feel secure in life. I think of those who have stood strong in their faith and have been such great examples to us. They are the men and women you want to follow. Our former pastors are those kind of people. They have showed us how to stand strong in the midst of a battle. They have never wavered in their faith. They have made such a big difference for us. In our life let's make sure we are the people that others want to follow. Let's make the difference others are looking for.

KEEP CHRIST IN VIEW 313

Growing up we didn't have cell phones. My dad and many farmers worked in the fields all day without anyway of letting someone know if they needed help. Most of us have become so dependent on our phones. If we can't find it, we become very concerned and will look everywhere until we find it. Personally I try to keep mine in a pocket or in plain view of where I am. We should be that desperate with Christ. We should always hold Him in close view; and never leave home without Him. If you can't find Him…He's right where you left Him.

SEEKING HELP 314

I finally had to purchase a new cell phone. Mine was old and worn out. My new phone was so different. There were a lot of new features I had to master. In fact I had to seek help from my niece. In life we try to "figure things out" that may seem confusing and we don't understand. Just as I had to have help for my phone, we must not be hesitant to seek help. Our best resource is to turn to God who has all the answers to life's questions. Don't try to figure it out alone. His desire is to "help in time of trouble". The good thing is He is available twenty-four hours a day.

ACT OF GOD

Recently I heard a true story of a man who sang in night-clubs. He got saved and told his manager he could not sing there anymore. His boss told him he had to continue singing because he had signed a contract. The only way he could get out of it was an "act of God". The singer replied "that's what I've been trying to tell you. When I got saved it was an act of God". His manager left the room. You and I have experienced many "acts of God": Salvation; healing; deliverance; and His protection… just to name a few. What a great transition that was!

WE ARE BLESSED

Many people do not like to celebrate birthdays. I'm one that likes the idea. I even tease and say I will celebrate the entire month if possible. I see every birthday as a day to count my blessings and see what God has done for me over the past year. Every day on earth is a "gift from God". I encourage each of us to rise up each morning thanking God for this day and what He has in store for us. Regardless of how we feel or what we are going thru; when we wake up in the morning or we lay our head to rest; we are blessed! This is the day the Lord hath made, we will rejoice and be glad in it.

HE'S WATCHING YOU

I heard on the radio how wonderful the "eye of an eagle" is. An eagle can see a fish in the water from several hundred feet away from flying above. They can see something the size of a rabbit at more than three miles away. God is so amazing. He can see you and me right where we are; any time of the day. Yet at the same time He can see someone else in another state or country. He also sees every tear that falls from our eyes. You see, the eagle has nothing over our Savior. His eyes are on the sparrow; and I know He watches me.

THE PROBLEM SOLVER 318

I'm the kind of person that likes to solve every problem. I guess it's because I want to be a help to others. But I have come to realize there are things that are out of my control. That's why I totally rely on Jesus to take care of things I can't. He's the solution to every problem. However, there are a couple things He can't do. He can't fail us and He can't lie. But think about all the things He can do. I know that "all things are possible with Him". The things that are impossible with man, are possible with God. He can solve every problem you and I may face. That's the wonderful God we serve.

HOP ON 319

We used to take our widows and sponsors to a friend's farm. We had so much fun out there. We would climb on a hay wagon to take a hayride. I watched those ladies climb on and I thought not one more person could get on that wagon-but I was wrong. Many wanted to take the "first ride" instead of waiting. It reminds me how we are getting ready for Heaven. Like the hayride there may be some bumps along the way; but we are waiting for more people to climb on board. On this trip to Heaven I encourage you to "hop on" . There's only a "first ride" to this destination.

OUR PROTECTION

Our first dog was our little watch dog. My husband's brother stayed with us for a while when he was going thru a tough time in his life. Late one night our dog heard him coming onto the porch and went to the front door barking. She was going to protect us. My husband was right behind her. When the door opened she ran behind my husband's legs peeping around. In life we face obstacles that at first we feel brave; but fear sets in and we want to hide. We must remember God is already ahead of us. It's good to know He is our protector and there's nothing to fear.

WHEN PIGS FLY

My dad always got little pigs that soon grew up to be big hogs. I told Mike if we lived in the country I wanted some hogs. He said we would get 100 acres; with our house being on the first acre and the hogs on the back of the 100 acres. I've heard the saying "when pigs fly" many times. It means something won't ever happen. Many feel like some things won't happen like a person's lifestyle; attitude; or the possibility of them being saved. But God doesn't see it that way. I believe all people can change because it's possible with God. This is where the saying "when pigs fly" ceases.

CHANGES

There are a lot of changes that occur in life. Time changes in the spring and the fall. Growing up life was more simple without the technology we have today. People change, wages change, population changes, even cars and homes change. But I am so thankful God doesn't change. He is always the same yesterday, today and forever. He doesn't follow the crowd; but desires the crowd to follow Him. Another change will occur when Christ comes back. Our bodies will be whole and our life will change. What an awesome transformation that will be.

PRACTICE WHAT WE PREACH 323

I never met my dad's parents; but heard much about them. Dad's mom was known in the community as a strong, devoted Christian woman. My dad and his dad found her under the apple tree dead, where she had been picking apples. The Newspaper put an article about her on the front page of the paper. It told about her love and devotion to God; as well as the community. What an awesome testimony. Sounds like she was a great witness to all she met. We should each strive for a testimony that will preach our funeral while we are still living.

CALMING THE STORM 324

My niece shared a text about how calm she felt just knowing her son was home and upstairs sleeping. She said even though he wasn't downstairs hanging out with her; she felt such peace knowing he was up there. In the middle of our storms; even if we don't see God or feel Him; we can have the same peace just knowing He is right there with us. The Bible tells of the disciples in a boat during a storm where Jesus was in the back of the boat asleep. They woke Him up with the words "don't you care we perish"? He got up, spoke peace and the winds were calm. He will do the same for you and me.

BE AN ENCOURAGEMENT

With things going on in this world; we can rest assured all is well….because God is in control. It's such a blessing when others call and encourage us. I've heard a saying that is true "what goes around comes around". I believe when we encourage or bless someone, those same words of blessing will come back to us. Being an encourager is so important in our Christian walk. Let's be the one to lift someone up and not put them down. When we rise up in the morning we should have the desire to find someone to encourage and bless. That person won't be disappointed; and neither will we.

LED BY GOD

I love to see horses out in a field grazing. Before I was born our family had a horse or two. My older sisters would sit on the horse while dad led the horse around. Dad would tell my sisters to "hold the reins". He knew they could get hurt if for any reason the horses took off running. The enemy would love to take us for "a ride" that would lead us to danger. Each of us must allow God to "hold the reins" and lead us along to "where the water's cool flow bathes the weary one's feet, God leads His dear children along".

BLESSINGS IN-BLESSINGS OUT

As a young girl I would go to town with dad on Saturdays. That was a big deal if you lived out in the country. Dad knew many people in town, so he would go and chat with them all. They were in the stores, police and sheriff's office; even in funeral homes. Didn't matter to me, because they all gave me coins. My sisters said I would come home with more money than I went with. That's like God. He blesses us coming in and going out. We all have been so blessed from unforeseen sources when we needed it most. Today count your blessings. You'll see what God has done.

TAKING THE FIRST STEP 328

When I was about one year old, I decided to try to walk. I was a "wee bit" chubby so it wasn't easy to take a step. But finally I took that step and more steps; and before long I was walking. I would fall; but my mom was assured I would be ok and if I fell I would get back up. My middle sister would walk behind me to make sure I didn't fall down. On our Christian journey we find it difficult to step out of our comfort zone to do what God wants us to do. I have found out after we take the first step the second one is much easier. It's called a walk of faith. The good thing is He walks with us. I would say He "has got our back".

NOT PERFECT 329

I remember the day I got baptized. It was in late October and I was fifteen years old. I never liked water but I remember I wasn't afraid. The water was brisk; but I was so excited. I remember how good I felt when I came up out of that water. You see the water didn't save me. I had taken care of that at an altar a few weeks before. But I did feel I had left the "old self" under that water. That's been many years ago; but it's still real in my mind. As I live each day I realize more and more that I am not perfect, but forgiven. By the way I wasn't the only one in that water-Jesus went in there with me.

AVOID SIN

I love to watch deer grazing out in the field. But we have had encounters with them that aren't so pleasant. Many years ago we were headed home from Arkansas when I hit a deer that totaled our car. Another time my husband hit a group of deer he couldn't avoid and totaled that car. That's like life. Like the deer, it seems things can pop up from no where. They can look innocent; but can bring much harm to us if we don't avoid it. The closer you get to it; the more dangerous it becomes. Sin can harm us or cripple our walk with God. Let's stay on guard every moment.

DRY, WEAK, AND FROZEN

A pastor gave an example of how Christians can become "lax or slack" in their walk with the Lord. He said they can become "dry as yesterday's bird nest; weak as last weeks tea; and as frozen as home-made ice cream". At a restaurant in another city a few years ago I ordered a half-roasted chicken. When they brought it to me, it was still frozen. Needless to say I sent it back. When we are cold, dry or weak as a child of God, it doesn't attract others to this walk of life. It fact it will turn them off. I encourage each of us to let the fire burn in us so others can see Jesus inside us.

COME ON IN

Our world really needs prayer. People are looking for peace and true happiness. There are those who are looking for "true love" and think they can find it in things. But I can assure you the only true joy, peace and love will be found in Jesus. A song was made popular years ago that said "People need the Lord… at the end of broken dreams, He's the open door". Many have traveled down many roads and opened many doors only to be disappointed. In fact their dreams have been shattered to pieces. If you are at your wit's end; I urge you to call out to Jesus. The door is standing open just for you.

UP AND DOWN 333

When I was young in elementary school, we would go outside to the playground for recess. A friend and I went to the "seesaw" or "teeter-totter". I would go up in the air while my friend would be on the ground. She would hold it down so I was stuck in the air. I did the same to her. People have a big influence on our life. They can lift us up, or they can let us down. Our spirits can be on cloud nine; and one jolt can bring us back down. I'm thankful God lifts us up. Our prayer should be "Lord lift me up and let me stand…Lord plant my feet on higher ground".

AN IMAGE TO REMEMBER 334

One day coming back from Florida, as we were crossing the Alabama line, something on the right caught our eye. It was a small white church with a hearse parked at the front door. There must have been 150 cars parked on the parking lot, the grass and the road. People were standing on the outside because there was no way to get in. I'm not sure if that person held a high position in that community; but I know he had made an impact on many people. That image is still in my mind. May we all make that impact on the lives of others. You see, one day we will enter Heaven. Jesus will be standing at the gate. That will be an image we won't ever forget.

THE HOLY SPIRIT IS WELCOME 335

One winter our family rented a cabin at a State Park. My mom, sister and I went on ahead to take supplies. We tried but couldn't get the fireplace to burn; and believe me it was very cold. When my husband got there, he got the fire going and it was great to feel the warm heat. Without the Holy Spirit in our life, we will become very uncomfortable in our walk with the Lord. In fact we will be miserable. We need the Holy Spirit in our life; our home; and in our churches. As one pastor said "the Holy Spirit can do more in 30 seconds than I can do in 30 minutes".

SUPERMAN-SUPERNATURAL 336

One day we took our widows to Metropolis Illinois to see Superman. There is a big statue of him there; and all the ladies enjoyed having their picture taken with him. This character was known for "super powers" he possessed. But Superman has nothing on our Savior. Christ has super powers no one else can comprehend. He can be everywhere at one time. He can hear millions of people at the same time. He knows what we are going to say before we speak. There is no one like Him. He's my "super-natural" hero for sure.

PASS AROUNDS 337

There's a restaurant I love going to called Lamberts in Sikeston MO. It makes a nice one-day trip and the food is great! This restaurant is known for their "throwed rolls". Right where you are sitting, they will throw you a roll. They also have "pass-around" food they add to your plate of food. One thing for sure you won't leave there hungry. In life we have things thrown at us that are not pleasant at all. But Jesus comes with blessings that He "passes around" to lift our spirits. Our plate is filled and we become so full with all the goodness of the Lord. It's a great place to feast for sure.

WE WILL WIN 338

Yesterday I was sitting in my car while my husband was inside seeing his doctor. Mike had been experiencing shortness of breath for a while. I sit there praying and remembering how God had always come thru for him. Sometimes when we are going thru things; we may feel we are out in "left-field" with the unexpected. If you are going thru a situation, you may feel the ball is not in your court. But God is a good referee watching every move we make. You know this is not our first ballgame. We've been there many times. As long as Christ is with us-we will win.

IT'S SPRING 339

Spring is one of my favorite seasons. After a cold, bitter, and snowy winter, it's refreshing to see the flowers blooming and the tree's budding. As I absorb it all, I can see new life everywhere.

Even the little birds seem excited with the change. That's the way it was when we got saved. The past was gone and replaced with SON-light. Everything looked beautiful and the world looked so much brighter. How does your world look today? I encourage you to give your life to Him and ask Jesus to forgive you. You will experience a new beginning in your life as well.

PROBLEM SOLVED 340

I'm the kind of person that likes to solve problems for myself and others. But I'm reminded I sometimes just can't do it. We think the answer is in money, things, or people; but in life we must go to our Heavenly Father for guidance. People say "I've tried everything; guess all I can do is go to God". That should be our first choice. I used to hear Dottie Rambo sing: "It's me again Lord, I got a problem I can't solve". The song goes on to say "I don't mean to bother you". Friend it's no bother. He wants us to come to Him at any time. It's the Father's good pleasure to solve any problem for us.

STAY PUT 341

Our family would go to the pond to fish. My mom would prepare a picnic lunch to eat before we fished. After we ate we would go down to the pond with our fishing poles. If the fish weren't biting, I would go to other places around the pond. I soon realized I should have stayed where I was. Some people feel they need to move to another location to receive from God. I have realized God will meet us right where we are. If we didn't feel Him, we can rest assured He was there all the time. The only move we need to make is closer to Him. That makes all the difference in the world.

BETTER THAN A STEAK 342

My husband and I went to a picnic area in the Smoky Mountains many years ago. Driving thru looking for a picnic table, we came to one area where a big bear was standing in the middle of the table eating big steaks the guys had grilled. Did you know that every time we are about to sit down at the table of the Lord to enjoy His blessings, the enemy tries to step in; distract us and try to steal our blessings? The sad thing, like the bear we let him do it. Satan comes to steal, kill and destroy; but Jesus comes to give us life-more abundantly. If you ask me, that's a lot better than a steak.

NOT IN A GARBAGE CAN 343

Several years ago our family stayed in a cabin in the Mountains. One night we heard a lot of noise on the porch. Looking out we saw raccoons trying to get into the garbage cans; trying to find some "treats". Many people are looking for things to satisfy what's missing in their life. Those people have looked in the wrong places. The enemy has "tricked" them by enticing them with other things. Like the raccoons, they are still looking for that missing ingredient. I encourage you to look to Jesus. What you are looking for is found in Him. I can guarantee you it won't be in a "garbage can".

MY SOUL IS THIRSTY 344

I have always loved to go to Fall Creek Falls State Park. There is one waterfall that is about 256 feet tall. I remember our family going there one year and the waterfall was not pretty at all. You see, there had been very little rain which affected the beauty of the waterfall. When we as Christians don't experience the "rain" of the Holy Spirit in our life, we become dry spiritually and we become miserable. We must sit in His presence every day. The Holy Spirit is like a "cleansing agent". It's like a "cool drink" of water in a dry land. "My soul thirsteth for God". Psalms 42:2

←——————————————→

THE ULTIMATE PRICE PAID   345

I love going to yard sales. I have found some great bargains there. "Someone's junk becomes another person's treasure" is so true. Several years ago we took our widows to a city yard sale in Watertown. It's amazing what we all came home with. Looking back, every Christian can say they traded some "junk" for some "treasures" in Heaven when they got saved. The junk we had was not anything we wanted or anyone else would want. Like the yard sale items, we had gotten tired of them. What we received from the Lord didn't cost anything. It was already paid for on Calvary.

←——————————————→

PRESSURE COOKER EXPERIENCE   346

Several years ago my husband bought me a pressure cooker; but I never used it. The old ones were known for accidents from the pressure; and the steam was dangerous. Now they are safe and there is a lot of benefits from using them for cooking. The food is tender, juicy and holds a lot of flavor. Some people are like the old pressure cookers. When they are under pressure they "blow up" and "let off steam" that can cause harm to others. As Christians, we should be a lot like the new pressure cooker: tender-hearted and flavored with the Holy Spirit. The next time you are under pressure, see which pressure cooker you are.

CURIOSITY

On one occasion my husband and I took our four nieces to Beech Bend Park. One of our nieces got a splinter in her finger. My husband was in the process of getting it out when the heads of all four girls was looking in at the procedure. It was funny because my husband could not see the splinter for their heads. People are a lot like that. They are full of curiosity. I've noticed people are curious about the things of God; but for some reason they are "skittish" and don't want to get involved. If you are one of those standing on the sidelines and never experienced the things of God; I encourage you to step in. Don't be a spectator; be a participator.

$$\longleftrightarrow$$

LISTEN TO THE RAIN

We have visited several Zoos over the years. I remember how tall the giraffes were and how large the elephants were. The Ark that Noah built had to be a big one to bring all those animals into it. Imagine how noisy and "stinky" it must have been. I admire him for building that ark; in spite of all the people that declared "it's not going to rain". But Noah took God at His word. Many sermons have been preached about Christ return; yet many do not believe it will happen. You can tell by the way they are living. Things are pointing to His return. The rain came in Noah's days; and Jesus will come also.

$$\longleftrightarrow$$

A SONG IN THE NIGHT

My husband and I used to do a lot of camping. We camped until it was too hard on my husband with his back issues. On one occasion we met a couple of teachers who invited us to their campsite. When we got there they picked up their guitar and began to sing a song they had written about us. It was a great night as we sat around the fire. God can give us a song in the middle of the night; in spite of what is going on in our life. "Some thru the waters; some thru the flood; some thru the fire; but all thru the blood. Some thru great sorrow God gives a song; in the night-season; and all the day long".

WHAT'S MISSING? 350

Have you put something in a "safe place" and went back and it wasn't there? Maybe it was your keys or an important paper. We say "I just had it, or I just put it there. Where could it have gone"? It's amazing how things can disappear. We back-track our steps hoping to have some remembrance of where it is. When I can't find something I have learned to stop, sit down and pray. It's amazing how some times I go back to that same place and it's there. With things going on in your life, have you lost your faith, joy or peace? Do you feel overwhelmed and wonder where you lost it? You will find everything missing in the presence of God.

THE MEAL GOES ON 351

When our widow's group was much smaller, we would plan a progressive meal for our ladies at different homes. The first house would serve an appetizer; the second soup; the third was the main course; and the last was the dessert and devotion. This was an event we all enjoyed. This reminds me of our walk with God. We progress as we draw closer to Him. The progression comes thru our prayer time, Bible study, and our fellowship with Christ. It's as good as the progressive meal; but like having dessert all the time; and you don't have to travel to partake of it.

— — →

I CAN'T FORGET IT   352

When Mike and I went to Washington DC, it was a trip of a lifetime. Many memories stand out in my mind from that one trip. The "Change of Guards" at Arlington Cemetery was astounding; but the visit to the Viet Nam Wall brought tears to our eyes. We watched as Viet Nam Veterans placed their hand on the name of a buddy; or a mom reaching out and touching the name of her child with tears falling off their cheeks. These paid a great price for our freedom; but one man who died that you and I can be free from sin, brings tears to my eyes. Some may forget, but Jesus is my hero. "I never shall forget the day and all the burdens of my soul was rolled away". That's what I call FREE.

← — — →

A CROSSROADS   353

On one of our travels, we came to a city called Bristol; a city straddling two states: Tennessee and Virginia. When you reach that point you must make a choice which way to go. One wrong turn can send you in the wrong direction. In our life there will be times when we face crossroads on this journey. A wrong move can cause disaster and destruction. It's important we choose the road that will lead us straight to Heaven. It may be a less traveled road, but I can guarantee we will get to where we are going if we follow the "road-signs" Christ has posted for us. We've come too far to turn back now.

THE ART OF FORGIVING

When Jesus was being persecuted He prayed "Father forgive them for they know not what they do". In so much pain He was willing to forgive those who treated Him so bad. Hanging between two thieves He heard the cry of one of the thieves and said "today thou shalt be with me in Paradise". No wonder he found it important to tell us to forgive those who do us wrong. We should be the "bigger person" and say "I forgive". I read where the tongue doesn't have one bone; yet it can break a heart. Proverbs 21:23 says "if we keep our tongue" it will keep us out of trouble. May we say "I forgive" or even more "please forgive me".

◄───────────────►

PRAISING JESUS

I have learned to praise the Lord for who He is; and everything He is to me. The Bible tells of a group of people who placed palm branches and clothes down for Jesus as He rode into Jerusalem on a colt. It was there that the crowd shouted "Hosanna-blessed is He that cometh in the name of the Lord". They recognized Him. Do we recognize His presence in the room or do we realize His presence resides in us? Do we take Him for granted? We may not use "palm branches" but we have two hands we can lift up in praise to Him. Today let's make a point of praising Him. "Let everything that hath breath, praise ye the Lord". You and I definitely qualify.

HE'S ALREADY BEEN THERE 356

I've heard many songs and sermons about Jesus and His death on the cross. It touches my heart to think that one man would be willing to take the abuse and pain; and even die a horrible death for everyone to have eternal life. I never get tired of the story; even though every time I hear it told, it can bring tears to my eyes. To think His blood was shed for our salvation; and the stripes He took was for our healing. He took all this intense pain and suffering to know what it feels like when we face obstacles in our life. Whatever you are going thru, just know He knows how you feel, because He's already been there.

←――――――――――→

PEACE LIKE A RIVER 357

During the heavy rain, I've looked out many times and watched as the limbs bend under the pressure. In life we face storms in our life, causing our strength to be drained and causing us to feel weak. When we feel we cannot take another step, it's then we feel the strength of the Lord restore us. When He speaks peace, the storm disappears. I'm thankful God has the control of the physical storms as well as the spiritual storms in our life. I read something that was so good: "God may let us bend; but He won't let us break". Rest assured God's got whatever you are facing in life. Stand strong on His promises.

←――――――――――→

AGAPE LOVE 358

Growing up I always enjoyed sitting at the table with the family enjoying a meal. I was thinking how Jesus was sitting at the table; the last meal He would have with His disciples before being crucified. I've often thought how He probably looked around that table with love; even though He knew one of them would betray Him and another would deny Him. How many of us have been slothful at sitting at the table with Him, our walk with Him, our Bible reading or our prayer time; yet He still loves us. I'm reminded how He looks beyond all our faults and sees our need. That's what we call "Agape Love".

←———————————→

THE CLEANING UP PROCESS   359

I always feel bad when I do something wrong. I always ask God to forgive me. Peter denied knowing Jesus three times; just like Jesus had told him. I can imagine how he felt when he heard the rooster crow; and seeing Jesus look at him. It says Peter wept bitterly. When we "mess up" or feel we have failed in some area of our life; it's important we feel the sadness of letting God down; but also knowing we serve a God who loves us and will forgive. Psalms 51 says "create in me a clean heart O God and renew a right spirit within me". When we pray that prayer, I can assure you He will do just that.

←———————————→

THIS MUCH!   360

My husband and I have talked about how our moms were always there when we got hurt. Mary, the mother of Jesus, must have shed many tears as she watched her son go thru so much. I am sure she wanted to embrace Him and make things better. While hanging on that cross and taking His last breath, I know that was an emotional time for her. Maybe you have a broken heart or even felt some fear creep into your life. Jesus knows exactly how you feel. He has come to "heal the broken hearted".

When He was on the cross, you and I were on His mind. Today come to Jesus He's waiting with open arms saying "I love you this much".

NO NEED TOO BIG 361

I often think how I miss family and friends who have gone on before us. I miss the laughs, the meals and other events we did together. The day after Jesus was crucified; I'm sure things did not seem right. Jesus, the one who had walked with them; taught them and healed them, was now gone. I'm sure everywhere they looked, it reminded them of Him. Is Jesus missing in your life? Is there an empty spot that nothing will fill? He's waiting for you to invite Him in. "Behold He stands at the door and knocks; if any man will open the door-He will come in". He's all you and I need.

SUNDAY'S COMING 362

I often think how those ladies went to the tomb to carry spices early that morning. I wonder what was going thru their mind and what their conversation was between them. Can you imagine their reaction when they saw the stone was rolled away and He was not in the grave? The angel assured them He was risen. It's exciting to know He is alive. Because He lives, you and I can face tomorrow. We may not know what tomorrow holds, but we do know who holds tomorrow. As my niece said a few days ago "Sunday is coming". So true it is. It's here and we have nothing to fear. Spread the word today. Jesus is alive today and forevermore.

THE LILY IN OUR VALLEY

363

I love going to the Mountains. We've gone to the top and have seen the tops of those mountains reaching toward the clouds. We love mountaintop experiences in our life. The valley is not as appealing to us. My husband says he looks for the beauty while he is in the valley; it's there you see what you don't see on the mountaintop; like beautiful flowers and growth. It's true that in the valley, He restores our soul. I can say for sure He can be the Lily in our valley. We just need to look around and see what God has to offer us while we are in the valley. We can experience "peace in the valley" for sure.

MORE THAN ENOUGH

364

What does it mean when we say we've had enough? It means we've had all we need to satisfy; or it could mean this is all we can handle. I heard a song that reminded me Jesus' presence is enough in every situation we face. The lyrics said "I've been thru enough to know He'll be enough for me". Stop and think about things we've gone thru. He was all we needed. I recall another song that says "He is more than enough to make a blind man to see…He's more than enough to guide you and me". "It hasn't entered into the heart of man the things which God has prepared for them that love Him". What more can we ask for?

ON BOTH ENDS OF THE LINE

365

A story on the news reminded me how God works in every situation. A couple and small son got caught in a flood. They hung on to the windshield wiper to keep from being swept away, as the mom prayed "God send someone to help us". A truck came by on their way to help another family. The truck stopped and a man jumped out. His words to her were "God sent me here". It was a prayer she had just prayed. In our situation He knows how to make things happen for us. He can use anything or anyone that comes our way to make it come to pass for us. All we have to do is cry out "Lord help us" and He will. He will work on both ends of the line.